IT C... GET BETTER THAN THIS

RANDY O'NEAL

Fulton Books
Meadville, PA

Published by Fulton Books 2024

ISBN 979-8-88982-300-1 (paperback)
ISBN 979-8-88982-301-8 (digital)

Printed in the United States of America

Foreword

RANDY O'NEAL IS AN enigma. Most people who know him know he loves his God, his family, his country, and his community. They know he is a good son, husband, father, grandfather, friend, citizen, employee, and employer; they know he lives out the faith he professes in actions, not just words. Many know Randy loves writing about all the facets of life and the people intertwined in his life story; when he writes (especially poetry), he dredges deep places and freely expresses what he finds there. As you read, you are likely to connect deeply; you may laugh hard or even cry.

He is not only an enigma; he is a "Renaissance man." Randy gardened and logged for long, hard hours as a teenager with his father, Bud O'Neal. He ran his dad's paper-wood business for a while after his dad began driving for Marshall Durbin Poultry Company. After high school graduation, Randy then began working for that same company as a dispatcher and was promoted to a company manager's position within three years. Here he attended many seminars at Auburn and Mississippi Universities. At Mississippi State during a poultry conference, he spoke from the podium to address over two hundred attendees. At one point, his company sent him to take the Dale Carnegie public speaking course. During his fifty-year employment, he and his wife, Jean, were also contract growers for Marshall Durbin.

Randy presently serves as Vice-President of the Washington County Historical Society, sits on the board of St. Stephens Historical Park (the first capital of the Alabama territory), chairs the ALDOT Safety Committee for Washington County, and is a board member of the Washington County Solid Waste Commission. He is a member of the Proverbial Pen writers group and a member of the Heart of Dixie Collectors Club. In past years, he has served as president of Chatom Middle School PTO and president of the Chatom City League Youth Football organization. In 2020, he was inducted into the Washington County Hall of Fame. The Jack and Maudeen Thompson Dixie Youth Baseball/Softball Field Complex in Chatom has one of its four fields named "O'Neal Field" for him and his family.

If that is not enough to support my designation of "Renaissance man" status, Randy has written many columns in the local paper in Chatom and surrounding counties. There is also a book of beautiful, poignant poems not yet published, although many have been read and loved at weddings, births, and other life-changing events. Anyone who is interested and involved in and pursues fervently and masters many things fits the definition!

It is important that you know not just Randy's works, accomplishments, and work ethic. I hope this tribute will reveal his very heart.

—Alice Richardson Grimes

The Glory Days
of Old Yarbo

THE STEAM WHISTLE FROM the Ingram-Day sawmill sharply broke the quiet spring morning, signaling another day of work and school. Already, smoke from the woodstoves through the old Yarbo town drifted from the houses as breakfast was prepared.

Soon the mill workers could be seen walking in the old dirt road with their lunch buckets full of biscuits and leftovers from supper the night before, ready for their daily tasks.

Boys and girls laughed and talked while on their way to the little red schoolhouse that sat upon the hill. Mrs. Mabry Ferguson stood in the schoolhouse door, ringing the bell and welcoming the children.

Another whistle blew, and the saws of the mill started their ever-familiar song that could be heard for two miles or more, letting everyone know that life around the mill was good. Nearly a hundred houses lined the intertwined roads where families lived and made their living in and around the Ingram-Day mill.

Mr. Harvison and Mr. Goldman visited on the bench beside the front entrance of the old store and greeted others who walked in. Inside the store, Mr. Jim Reynolds stocked his shelves with all things most would need without having to venture out of town to buy, such as canned food, clothes, shoes, cloth material, and the like. Jars full of jelly beans and rock candy were displayed to catch the eye of the boys and girls while moms and dads shopped. Mr. Jones pulled up in his horse-drawn wagon for some mule feed and other supplies needed for home. Mr. Willie Ferguson drove up in his old, rattling, stake-bodied Model T truck, loaded with turpentine barrels to fill up with gas at 11 cents a gallon. The pump was operated by hand-cranking five gallons of gas up into the clear cistern, then draining it into the truck.

The train from Ellisville logging camp blew its whistle as it crossed Road 17 to signal any approaching traffic and to let the mill know another load of logs was coming in. The train stopped by the millpond and rolled its logs into the water where they floated until they were pulled up into the mill for sawing. The logs were sawed up mostly into huge timbers and lumber.

The noon whistle blew for lunch, and the whir of the saws was silenced while the men ate their treats from their lunch buckets and tried to find shade for a few minutes of relaxation before returning to work. In the evening, the saws were silenced again, ending another long day of toil.

Children had already left the little red schoolhouse and were beginning their evening activities. Some of the townspeople took an evening stroll through the town park that sat adjacent to the old store. Wisteria blooms that covered the huge arbor at the entrance of the park provided a sweet, fragrant invitation to the many attractive displays inside the park. A teenage boy and girl sat on the side of the octagonal-shaped goldfish pond, holding hands as they made a date for the weekend to go to the town's theater. Birds sang as the evening lingered, enhancing the enjoyment of the afternoon strolls.

Smoke again drifted from the houses that lined the dirt road as wives prepared the evening meals. The aroma of woodstoves cooking fried chicken, pork chops, vegetables with cornbread, and biscuits beckoned hungry appetites.

Blows from axes could be heard as the men of the house split wood and chopped splinters to fill boxes and be used the next day for the stoves and fireplaces. Boys played kickball in the dirt road while the girls played hopscotch in the smooth, grass-free front yards of the houses as the sun sank behind the loblolly pines and water oaks. Mothers soon called the children in from their play as coal-oil lamps were lit inside the homes. The children worked on their next day's lessons while their parents listened to Edward R. Murrow report on the status of World War II on the radio.

In the middle of the morning of August 14, 1945, the mill whistle began blowing and blowing and blowing. Everyone knew this was highly unusual, so they congregated at the old store located directly across the railroad track from the sawmill to see what had happened.

It was announced that the war had ended! The mill shut down because the government was its biggest customer, and most of it was dismantled and moved to the local E. L. Jordan mill. Most of Yarbo's people left for other jobs, and the settlement slowly dwindled away.

There are still several families there today who have memories and tales of that era. Beneath the thick underbrush, one can see the concrete front of the old store where the gas pump stood and some of the outlines of roads and fence lines of some of the yards of the houses. The old goldfish pond still sits as it was left many years ago in silent homage of life and times of the old Yarbo town.

Ol' Red

I WAS BORN IN 1948 in the town of Yarbo and had two of the best parents and six brothers and sisters that anyone could have. Because I was the youngest, I guess one could say that I had it made. They all took care of me, but I wasn't spoiled. My parents taught us to work hard and be respectful toward them and other people that we came in contact with.

Being respectful was something that they didn't have to make a point of teaching us; it came naturally. They set examples in their daily lives, and we followed them.

Whippings with a belt or strap were few, but they were handed out if the need came around. I never remember getting a whipping from Daddy, but Mama would hand out a swat on my rump if she thought I needed it to get in a little more of a hurry than I was in at that particular time.

As I said, I respected my parents, but there is still one thing I cannot believe to this day that I did.

I was in the living room watching TV, and Mama told me she needed me to walk down to Reynolds' store and pick up a few groceries for her. When she asked me, I replied, "Yes, ma'am," and continued watching the TV show. I was planning on going as soon as the show was over, but that wasn't fast enough for her. She came in there, and I thought she was going to swat me. For some reason, I reached down into a shoeshine box, came up with a brush, and flung it in her direction. As I was doing this, my mind was asking, "What in the world are you doing?" Well, the brush missed Mama and was heading toward the big, round dresser mirror of hers.

As it was heading toward the mirror, I kind of watched my life flash before my eyes. It is amazing how many things your mind can think of in a second: *Can I catch it? This ain't going to be good. Will I go to jail? Can I jump out the window?*

The brush hit the mirror and broke it. Mama stood there, stunned that I would do such a thing, and I must say, I was as stunned as she was. Then she picked up a belt, and I was already jumping up and down and screaming and hollering as she grabbed my arm. I was running around in circles while she was holding me, all the while tearing my tail up.

Now Mama had done this enough times with my other brothers and sisters that she could follow me around and still get in some pretty good pops with the belt. When she turned me loose, I ran all the way to the store, got the groceries, and ran back. When the mirror broke, there was one big piece, nearly half, that did not break, and I finished growing up with that piece sitting on the dresser as a reminder of one of the worst whippings I ever got.

I wasn't scared of Mama and Daddy. I respected them. But there was one thing around our household that did scare me. Big Red was an old red rooster that ran loose around the house, as all the chickens did, and he was, I supposed, the ruler of the yard. He was scared of Mama and Daddy, but he thought he had just as much right to do what he wanted to do as we kids did.

Big Red had a spur on each leg that appeared to be about two inches long and was very sharp. He used them to fight other roosters in the yard, and he would use them on you if he got half a chance.

We didn't get inside facilities until about the mid-1950s. Before then, we had an outhouse about thirty yards away from our back door. If I had to go to the bathroom out there, I would wait until Red was around toward the front of the house and then make a run for it. I would think Red wasn't watching me, but he was. I guess he was giving me a sporting chance to make it. I would take off running, and about halfway to the toilet, I would hear Red's wings flapping right behind me. Whew! Made it again!

But the show wasn't over yet. When I would get ready to leave, I would have to peek through a crack in the door and see where he was to decide when to make a run for the back door again. Red wasn't as aggressive if I had a stick in my hand, but I still didn't feel too confident even with the stick. I would shudder to think what would happen to me if I had hit him with the stick and killed him; Mama wouldn't have been too happy about that.

Now here is my redneck joke: "If the only thing to keep you from going to the bathroom is thirty yards and a red rooster, then you might be a redneck." I thought that one up myself!

Wash Day

AS I LEAVE MY house each morning, I always notice Mama's old, black washpot at the foot of my back steps and reminisce of times long ago. That same washpot used to heat the water that washed all our family's clothes now holds some beautiful day lilies. I can remember the smell of the lighter wood splinters being used to start the fire. Small sticks of oakwood were added along to keep the fire going. Water was drawn from the dug well by our back porch, then added to the pot. After the water was heated, it was transferred into a metal washtub which held a scrubboard. Mama would add soap to the water and then rub the clothes against the corrugated board to scrub them clean. They were then transferred to a clean tub of water for rinsing. I always enjoyed going to the automatic solar dryer to help Mama hang out the clothes. The solar dryer was two T bars about thirty feet apart with several pieces of wire stretched between them. As I got older, she would send me to do it by myself, which was not too much fun then.

The warm sun and breeze would have the clothes dried by the middle of the afternoon. I remember how nice the warm, dry clothes would smell as we were gathering them and putting them in the clothes hamper. If you were not a child back in the day and didn't experience running through a clothesline full of clean, white dried sheets while they were blowing in the breeze, then you surely missed a special time.

In time, Mama purchased a Maytag "wringer washer," which was so cool. Mama could wash clothes in any weather because everything was done inside. There was no more heating the water because by this time, we already had hot, running water. There were connecting hoses used to run the hot water into the washer. The neat thing then was the ringer that was used to squeeze the water out of the clothes. Mama was an expert at feeding the clothes into this. There were two rolling cylinders that were so very close together that you couldn't stick a piece of paper through. Mama could flip clothes into it like an expert. I tried it and got my fingers and hands caught several times. I finally gave up and let her do that task.

In later years, while working at Marshall Durbin, Mama put all the money she made there on an automatic washer and dryer from Sheffield's Furniture and Appliance Store. This shortened her workload further. Simply load the clothes in the washer, set the dial, and forget it until the cycle was finished. Then transfer the clothes from the washer to the dryer and set that dial. When the clothes were dry, the buzzer would sound, and the task was done. She could then wash and dry a load of clothes in a fraction of the time that it took using the old washpot; how good can it get?

I spoke to some ladies recently and asked them about a washer that would dry clothes also. I was told that there was something out there, but it was not reliable. We've advanced in so many other areas, but the housewife hasn't had much help with these washing and drying duties. I know my mama probably said each time of advancement from the washpot days, "It can't get any better than this," but in time it did. I would think that from that time that the first automatic washer and dryer were introduced, technology would be more advanced than it is now. If, and when, it does become more advanced, I will be amazed, but as I walk down my back steps every morning and see that old washpot, I will still appreciate and be amazed at what my mama went through on the day of the week called wash day.

Mama Was a Sharpshooter

I REMEMBER MY DAD was gone practically every workday all through the week. He worked at different places out in the logging woods with no means of communications of any kind. It was my mother's responsibility to keep the household intact, no matter what came up, until Daddy returned home in the late afternoon. With as many as four kids there during the day, there was always a good chance an emergency would come up from time to time that she would have to take care of. Now Mama didn't drive, and it wouldn't have done any good anyway because the only vehicle we had was Daddy's work truck that he took with him each day.

Mama was a pretty good nurse and could fix most cuts and abrasions with some rubbing alcohol, first aid salve, etc. We kids weren't too accident-prone, and if we did get hurt doing something we weren't supposed to be doing, we just kind of sucked it up and said nothing about it because alcohol burned like heck.

Most other women in the area were just like my mom and had the same responsibilities with keeping their households up during the day. They had to be pretty good at a lot of skills. As it turned out, Mama was pretty good with a rifle. I imagine there are many women today that are scared of guns for good reason. During the '50s, women needed to know how to use one. We kids were outside playing one day after lunch, just having a great time. Someone noticed a strange dog coming up the lane not acting just right. As a matter of fact, he was foaming at the mouth, shaking his head, and making noises. It was a strange dog to us as we had never seen this dog before. We took off to the front door of the house and began yelling for Mama. The dog stood in the yard for a little while, acting crazy, and then started running circles around the house. We were scared, but Mama wasn't. She retrieved the .22-caliber single-shot rifle that was always kept close by and slipped in a short .22 bullet. She then went to the front porch and stood by the slightly opened screen door. Now I don't want to be too descriptive to you animal-lover readers, but after the dog had made about five rounds, he was unable to make number 6; Mama took care of that one. She said the dog probably had gone mad from rabies as many dogs failed to get their rabies vaccination shots back then, and there were dogs that didn't really belong to anyone, just roaming about freely. We were happy to get to go outside again after the dog met his demise, but we didn't play around in front of the house just in case he happened to revive back up. Daddy arrived home that evening, and we all ran out to tell him about what happened and praised Mama on how good a shot she was with the .22. Yep, Mama was a sharpshooter!

Vacation Bible School

SUMMERTIME—THE SEASON ALL KIDS look forward to all year. Going to the beach and vacationing, along with spending time with grandparents, is on most kids' agendas. But there is another school so many kids will be attending during summer break…VACATION BIBLE SCHOOL!

As soon as school is out, one can already see signs in front of so many churches listing the dates for their vacation Bible schools. I remember around sixty years ago when I attended my church's Bible school at Spring Hill Baptist Church, located a few miles north of Chatom. Seems like yesterday when all the kids lined up outside the front of the church, standing with our teacher in formation and marching in behind the Christian and United States flags. After we were all in, we would pledge allegiance to each flag and then be seated. After a few words from our preacher, Brother William Ponder, we would all go to our respective classes. I always looked forward to listening to stories from our teacher about Jesus's life and how he loved us. Next we would get into arts and crafts and make a mess with our finger painting on paper plates and such. The ladies of the church that served as our teachers, as I remember, were Ms. Gracie Carpenter, Lelia Beech, Hazel Ferguson, Ella Dixon, and Bessie Singleton. I am sure there were more, but they escape my memory at this time; after all, it has been sixty years or so.

There is one thing we all looked forward to, and that was REFRESHMENT TIME! I remember finger sandwiches, homemade cookies, and plenty of Kool-Aid! If we were extra good, we would have ice cream and cake! There was always plenty, and everyone enjoyed these treats. But there was one time that really stuck in my memory.

My good longtime pal Bobby Carpenter and I had somehow decided to have a contest on how many of those little red solo cups of grape-flavored Kool-Aid we could drink. I don't remember which one of us came up with the idea, but we quickly set in to downing this delicious thirst-quenching drink. Before long, we were into the teens and working toward the twenties. I don't think we ever got to the twenties because we were quickly getting full. I would look at him, and he would look at me, turn another cup up, and down the hatch. It took longer and longer as it was getting harder to swallow this now not-so-delicious drink. I noticed I quickly began feeling not so well and headed toward the door leading to the outside. A few feet outside of the building, I started to hold my head over, and the not-so-delicious grape Kool-Aid began spewing from my mouth. I could see Bobby out of my periphery doing the same thing. Before it was over with, I had Kool-Aid coming out of my mouth, nose, and I do believe my ears also. It was so much that I would bet it was more than I had consumed. Bobby and I made a pact after that not to do any more of these stunts. From that day to this, I am not fond of anything grape-flavored. I miss those times of my childhood and still think of them when I see these signs in front of churches: VACATION BIBLE SCHOOL.

Riding on Our Mule Was Fun, but *Not* Cool

MULES HAVE BEEN USED for centuries as multitask animals. They were used, at times, as personal transportation and also to pull the family wagon. Teams of mules could be harnessed together to pull extremely large pieces of farm equipment, such as plows and combines.

Our mule, Ole Dick, was no exception. Dick's main job for Daddy's paper wood business was to pull the sawed-down trees from the stump to the landing to be cut up into smaller pieces for loading. On the weekends, he would be brought home if we needed him to plow our fields. If the location we were cutting was ten miles or so from home, we would haul him on the back of our Chevy pickup where Dick could be fed and watered without Daddy having to drive too awfully far back into the woods.

If, however, the location was closer, it was my illustrious job to ride Dick from there to our house on Friday after work and then back again on Sunday afternoon. I really didn't mind doing this unless it happened to cut into our gang's Sunday after-church and after-dinner ball game.

Preparing Dick for the trip was an easy task; putting his bridle on and throwing an old burlap sack across his back were all I needed to do. I remember we had an old military saddle, but it looked kind of awkward sitting on the back of an old gray mule. Dick was also quite tall, so I would lead him up beside the fence for me to climb on to make it easier for me to get onto his back.

13

Daddy would drive on up ahead of me to a point just before getting out of sight and pull over and wait until I passed him. About the time I was about to get out of his sight, he would pass me and keep doing this until we arrived at our location of work.

Ol' Dick really took his time while walking; he definitely didn't want to get in much of a hurry. This gave me a chance to observe things along the way that I wouldn't ordinarily have noticed if I was riding by in a car. I enjoyed listening to the sounds around me, such as birds singing and squirrels chattering. Occasionally I would see a raccoon or possum cross the road in front of me. If the sun was going down and darkness was approaching, Dick would perk up his ears if he thought he heard a booger that might be lurking in the bushes. I guess I was about as observant as he was.

On this particular afternoon, I remember we had to take Dick out to a location past the Barlow community. This was several miles from home, but not too awfully far for me to ride him. After we were on our way, I got to thinking that I would be passing by the houses where two pretty young ladies lived next door to each other. I was looking forward to passing by, thinking I may get a chance to see them and maybe wave if they happened to be outside.

As I got closer, I was getting a little nervous that if I waved, they may not wave back, and I would be embarrassed. Then I started wondering, *What pretty girl would want to wave at a little redneck boy riding by on an old gray mule?* As we were on our trek, I would be passed by older boys in their Fords and Chevys. Ol' Dick's coat was dirty, definitely nothing close as compared to a black thoroughbred horse. Dick's backbone was sticking up about an inch above the rest of him, and I was finding it quite uncomfortable because the corn sack didn't provide much of a cushion. It was getting hard for me to sit up straight, and I had to switch from one side of my behind to the other to share the pain.

I had it made up in my mind that I would have to look as good as I could. Ol' Dick wouldn't even try to hold his ears up straight. He would point his right ear up and his left ear straight out to the side and every now and then switch them. He wasn't helping me one bit trying to look presentable as we were getting close to the girls' houses.

I had holes in the knees of my Levi jeans, and my shirt had the sleeves cut off. Being barefoot and wearing an old cap with turpentine on, it didn't help matters either.

As I got closer, I was getting nervous that I might see the girls if they were outside, and they may not even notice me as I went by. I decided that I was going to sit up straight despite the pain radiating up from my backside and try to look as impressive as I could. As I passed by their houses, I looked and looked but did not see the first sign of them. I was disappointed but at the same time a little relieved. I figured out one thing that day, though: no matter how straight I tried to sit or how much I tried to get Ol' Dick to keep his ears straight, it's hard to look COOL on a MULE!

Sugarcane-Syrup-Making Day

THE SUN PEEKS OVER the horizon on a cool, crisp October morning in South Alabama, and sunlight kisses the tops of the tall Southern pines. Already, preparations are being made for a big day of making Southern sugarcane syrup. The smoke rises from the firepit at the syrup-making shed at Uncle Matt Carpenter's homestead. Ol' Jim, Uncle Matt's mule, is harnessed, and the singletree is hooked to a long pole that runs across the top of the metal juice-extracting mill that sits on top of the pedestal.

Soon neighbors began arriving to help as syrup-making requires several people to assist in getting this delicacy made. Syrup-making day is something that everyone in the surrounding area looks forward to because it is a good time to visit and possibly get to sample some of the sweet cane juice before it goes into the cauldron. Now, friends, this juice is something that sometimes doesn't sit well with everyone's stomach. A few years ago, I visited a place where syrup was being made and was offered some of this sweet treat. It was delicious, but the rest of the story is that for the next several days, I was reluctant to leave the house, if you know what I mean. I recently talked to one young lady who lived down the road close to Uncle Matt's. On syrup-making day, her dad would walk down the sandy dirt road with her and her little sister to where the syrup was being made. She said she and her little sister would try to run and skip on ahead of their dad in anticipation of arriving at the syrup shed. Men, women, and children were all welcome to come and help or just visit. It truly was

16

the place to be. Aunt Mamie Carpenter always had plenty of hot coffee and tea cakes for everyone.

Ol' Jim starts on the first of what will be several hundred circular trips as the pole turns the gears in the mill. One person feeds the long stalks of sugarcane into the mill. As the juice is squeezed out, it pours into a bucket, which is then moved over to the cooking pan above the fire in the brick pit. It was most important not to get the juice too hot, or it would scorch and be ruined. From what I researched, the cooking temp would be between 212 and 215 degrees. It took knowledge handed down from generation to generation to know how to do this expertly. As the juice was cooked, impurities would float and then be skimmed from the top of the cooking liquid. Uncle Matt and his assistants could tell by the minutes cooked and the color changing of the syrup when it was time to cool the fire and drain the syrup into a quart or half-gallon buckets. I am told that when it had time to cool, it was ready to be sampled. My research tells me that for every 120 gallons of juice cooked, only about 18 or 19 gallons of syrup is derived.

In current times, syrup making still goes on, but they don't do it like it was done in the good old days. Electric motors turn the gears to squeeze the cane. The cane juice is cooked in a very controlled environment and heated with butane burners to exactly control the temperature. Hydrometers are used to test the viscosity to tell when the syrup is done. All this is done inside an enclosed building with no visitors. Now how much fun is that?

I Wasn't Always
a Tenderfoot

BUT EVEN AS A boy, there were limits to my toughness.

On a recent night, I had to walk out to my pickup to remove the keys before retiring. The vehicle was parked in my driveway only a few feet from the garage, and I was in my sock feet, figuring I wouldn't need any shoes.

Walking across the smooth garage floor, I could feel some of the sand under my feet, which wasn't bothersome. But suddenly, I nearly went to my knees from stepping on an acorn that had somehow found its way into my garage. I knew then that I may have made the wrong decision about going barefoot. I was over halfway there, so I proceeded.

The roughness of the driveway cement caused me to walk more gingerly to my destination. I then returned to the soft indoor/out-door carpet in my basement, which was so comforting to my feet. I quickly realized I had become a tenderfoot, which was, in my earlier days, something you didn't want to be called by your pals.

There was a time, however, when going without shoes was commonplace. I recently came across a school picture of a class of fourth-graders from the 1950s and noticed that only a few of the kids were wearing shoes. I remember one spring, Ms. Turner, my third-grade teacher, said we could go barefoot at recess if we brought a letter from home giving permission. I forgot my note, so I decided I would write one myself and sign my mother's name.

After the first three pops from Mrs. Turner's paddle, I quickly knew I had made the wrong decision. It seemed very evident my penmanship was not as good as my mother's.

My mom had a rule that we kids couldn't go barefoot until the first of May. She said it took this long for the ground to get warm enough to keep us from catching cold. Her reasoning was based on an incident from years before, when she said an old man came to help Daddy flat-break the fields. It was in March or early April, I guess, and the ground was still cold and damp. The old man slid off his shoes and followed the mule while walking barefoot in the plowed furrow. He evidently caught a bad cold from this, which turned into something else, and in a few weeks passed away from his sickness.

When I was about eight years old, Mama began sending me down the road to the store for groceries and other items. The asphalt in the summertime on Highway 17 would get so hot that you could literally fry the proverbial egg. But that didn't stop me from going barefoot to Mr. Jim Reynold's store a couple of hundred yards from my house.

Sand spurs grew in abundance beside the highway during the hot days of summer. I knew when I left the warm sand of our dirt drive that I would have to run as far as I could and for as long as I could stand the burning pain from the hot asphalt. When the pain became intense, I would have to step into the grass for a minute to recover from the burning of my bare feet. The waiting sand spurs hid among the weeds and grass and added increased pain if their barbed spikes sank into this little country boy's burning feet. These things hurt!

After I stepped on one, I was in real trouble. In order to remove it, I didn't dare sit down on the grass and chance getting another one or two in my rear; I surely couldn't sit down on the two-hundred-de-gree blacktop and burn my rear there. So that left me trying to balance on one foot and trying to avoid hopping around and stepping on another spur with my good foot while painfully extracting the barbed, peanut-sized spur. Got it!

Then I had to make up my mind that, whatever the pain from the heated pavement, I would have to run all the way to the waiting shade of the canopy at the store.

The old pine-board bench, worn smooth over the years by resting patrons, provided comfort to my backside while the cool sand gave aid to my aching feet as I buried them underneath. Ahhhh!

Now for the reward. The shiny quarter I had in my cutoff jeans pocket was enough to buy my favorite treat, a banana flip and a king-sized Coke. After doing this hundreds of times, I already knew the cost. Ms. Gracie didn't have to tell me how much as I slid my quarter across the counter, money I had earned picking up empty Coke bottles. Returning outside to the shaded bench, I sat down and enjoyed this little piece of heaven in my life as the cold drink and sweet treat gave me renewed energy.

After I had rested and enjoyed my treat, I returned inside to pick up the things Mama had sent me to get and told Ms. Gracie to "charge it." I wished her a good day, walked outside the old country store with a brown paper sack of groceries on my hip, and stared at the heat radiating off Highway 17. Maybe shoes wouldn't have been such a bad idea after all.

Friday Sweets

WE HAVE THOSE DELICIOUS, and weight-depositing, Little Debbie oatmeal cakes that are always placed in an out-of-the-way location in our kitchen cabinets. Sitting alongside are always two packs of Dove's dark chocolate, one plain and one with almonds. My wife tells me that the chocolate is purely for medicinal purposes only. I think she inventories them often to make sure I don't overdo my intake of these delicacies.

I do know several of our friends' families whose stockpile of the likes far exceed ours. I was thinking the other day about how different things are now compared to how they used to be.

I remember when, at our house, Mama didn't keep the likes of the inventories as we have now. On Sundays we may have a cake for dessert, and Monday or Tuesday was as long as it would last. During the week, the sweets that were around were small. But on Friday, we kids knew what was coming: Daddy would always bring home a small paper bag of candy and treats from Mr. Mack McKinley's store in Chatom. The bag would contain peanut butter logs, suckers, bubble gum, hard rock candy, and the like. This was something we kids always looked forward to. On Friday evenings, my two older sisters, Peggy and Bonnie, and I would wait with anticipation for Daddy to come in from work with our treats. The only thing was, they were bigger than I was and always got to Daddy first and got first choice. Poor little Randy would end up with whatever was left. So that left me to come up with something to make sure I got my fair share. I finally figured out a way for me to be sure they couldn't beat me to the best of the candy.

The front door to our house had a wooden door on the inside and screen door on the outside. The screen door had a hook-type latch on it that was hardly ever fastened. I figured out that if I would latch the door, it would keep my sisters from getting ahead of me. I was so proud of myself and kind of smiled about my ingenious mind figuring this out. As I write this, I am running through my mind and trying to remember the last time I saw a screen door on a house; can't think of any at the present. Back in the day, not all houses had air conditioners. There would be a window somewhere in the house with a box fan sitting in the window pulling fresh air through. The screen doors would let fresh air pull through and at the same time keep flies and mosquitoes out; my, how times change. Sorry, back to my story.

I put my plan into action about thirty minutes before Daddy's time to arrive home. I giggled under my breath thinking about how cool my plan was. In the meantime, Mama had sent me to my room to clean it up, and I guess I was involved in my chore and forgot about the time. Suddenly I heard the door slam on Daddy's truck and immediately struck out running to meet him. I noticed as I sailed through the kitchen that my sisters were just getting up from the kitchen table. I think Mama had them peeling potatoes for supper, and while listening to the radio, they didn't hear the door slam. I was ahead of them now, and my hair was blowing in the wind on my race to meet Daddy. I was thinking about how fast I could run and had a huge head start on our race. As I was going through the living room, I held out my hands to push the screen door open as I ran past. When I was about a half-step away, my eye saw a terrible sight. I thought, *Somebody latched that door!* There was no way I could stop this speed I had built up. I tried to protect my head as I hit the screen door. Part of my head caught the cross brace, but the rest of me went through the rusted screen with me finally landing in a crumpled heap on the porch. That's when I suddenly remembered that I was the one who had latched the door.

My two giggling sisters unlatched the door and ran toward Daddy. Mama had already grabbed her switch and was striping my legs because I had demolished her screen door. I was trying to explain to her that Peggy or Bonnie must have been the ones that had latched it, and she should be whipping them; she wasn't buying any of that but did finally turn me loose. I ran to Daddy for sympathy and to see if anything was left for me in the little brown bag. My daddy had looked out for me and had saved me plenty. Isn't it something, how quickly emotions can change? I had gone from happy to hurt to being hurt worse and back to happy again in a few short moments. I guess life is full of changes. I hope yours are for the better.

Memories of the Old Lumber Mill Store

DURING THE DAYS OF Ingram and Day Lumber Mill, the town of Yarbo flourished around it. To serve the community, a commissary was built in downtown Yarbo, where it remained until well after World War II, and the mill, as well as a great many of the townspeople had left.

Mr. Jim Reynolds purchased the commissary building and business and ran it there for several years. In time, as the business had dropped off, Mr. Jim decided to rebuild the store over on Highway 17, which wasn't too far from where the store was originally built.

Several weeks after the store had been moved, a bunch of us neighboring kids, including two of my sisters, Peggy and Bonnie, were taking a stroll through the old town. The park was still there, so we walked and played around the octagonal-shaped fountain and among the huge crepe myrtles that grew in the park. After we left the park, we noticed the old store still standing there with the two large front doors swung wide open. We thought we would venture over there and take a walk inside to see how the old store looked after all the dry goods and stock had been removed from the shelves. The post office was also located in the store, with the abandoned boxes sitting there as if they were lonesome for some mail.

The old glass-fronted display cases had empty boxes of different sizes sitting helter-skelter along the shelves. Someone went behind the counter and, while pilfering through the boxes, let out a shout. We thought he had put his hand on a spider or something, and we rushed to see what he had. We couldn't believe what we had found. There, sitting among the empty boxes, were several boxes of candy bars that apparently had been overlooked during the moving. Wow. We quickly convinced ourselves that it was okay to take the candy as it has been a few weeks since the move.

Excited with such a find, we began filling our pockets and made a pact that we wouldn't tell anybody about it. We soon left with our cache and walked up the railroad bed, enjoying our new snacks. Before we had gotten too far, somebody said, "These things don't taste too good." Somebody else said, "Mine either." We stopped and started examining our delicacy more closely to quickly find the trouble. The candy bars had turned a different color than what they were supposed to be. Upon closer inspection, we found some tiny little bugs crawling around in them. URGHHHH!

We started spitting, gagging, and coughing, trying to throw up what we had already swallowed. Some of us were down on our knees, and others had their finger down their throat, trying to throw up. Had we been poisoned? Were we going to die? Eventually recovering, we started walking up the railroad bed again, swearing for the second time not to tell anybody about what we had gotten into.

I guess the old adage held true: "If something seems too good to be true, it usually is."

I Can Still Hear Minnie's "Howwwdeee" and Taste the Dangerously Hot Coffee

WITH NOT TOO MANY exciting things to do back in the 1950s and 1960s, country folks would break up the monotony of a dull week by visiting their neighbors after a long day's work and supper had been eaten.

Wednesday nights were for prayer meeting at church, so on a Tuesday or Thursday night, our family would load up in the old Chevy and visit a neighbor or some of our relatives.

We kids were always eager to go visit our cousins to enjoy an evening of play. The older folks usually sat on the front porch in rockers and swings, talking mostly of the weather and local news. It was common for the radio to be on in the window, tuned to some country music show. The program would usually feature such entertainers as Kitty Wells, Patsy Cline, Faron Young, Hank Williams, Ernest Tubb, Little Jimmy Dickens, and the beloved Minnie Pearl with her usual "Howwwdeee!" I know so many of you have never heard of these people, and some of you, I'm sure, are wondering why I failed to name your favorite singer of that era.

The lady of the house would usually have some leftover sweets to serve guests, but most of all, there was always plenty of hot coffee. Let me enlighten some of you who aren't familiar with the way coffee was made and served back then. There weren't any automatic coffee makers as we have today. Mostly, it was made by grinding coffee beans purchased from the store. The beans were poured into a hand-cranked grinder, which was a common fixture in kitchens during that time. The grounds were put in a coffeepot and boiled on the stove for a time suitable to get the acquired taste. This coffee was stout enough to curl your toes, but that is what most people liked. The coffee was boiled to about 5,000 degrees, or so it seemed, because there was no thermostat to regulate the temp. The strong aroma served as a good indicator that it was on its way.

Back then, no one would think of serving coffee without a saucer, and one didn't dare stick his lips to a coffee cup for the first sip. A good sip of unchecked coffee could maim one's tongue for life; the old saying is that it would "burn the hair off your tongue." The correct way was to pour a little of the coffee into the saucer, swirl it around a little for cooling, and then give it a good, long slurp. This was repeated several times until the coffee in the cup dropped to a temp that one could handle, usually about half of a cup.

The chirping crickets and calls from the distant whippoorwills provided relaxing nightly sounds. We kids would play tag or chase around the house and down into the edge of the woods or up the dirt drive. We would run until we got tired or someone got hurt by stubbing his toe on a tree root or some discarded car wheel in the grass. Running barefoot always did have some drawbacks.

Other games we played were three tin cans, red rover, and red light. Sometimes, if it was summer, we would catch fireflies and put them in a mason jar. Daddy always said they were very polite because they would show you their rear ends and give you a light to see it by; he always had humorous sayings for things.

When the coffeepot was empty, my parents would bid our friends good night, and then we would all load back into the old Chevy and return home, looking forward to our next visit. Life was a little slower, and friends and neighbors took time to visit one another. I sure do miss those times and will always have these fond memories.

Fond Fishing Memories

FISHING BACK IN THE 1950s was as much fun then as it is today, I guess. But it seems that it was a lot different than it is now.

Today, everyone has high-dollar equipment to enable them to catch more fish. In this modern age, people think they must spend thousands of dollars on rods, reels, big bass boats and depth finders, and also a big, new, jacked-up, four-door, four-wheel-drive, diesel pickup truck. The same '49 Chevy car that we used to go to church, get groceries, or go visiting in was the same one we used for fishing; just let the rear window down and slide the poles through until they reached the floorboard, and we were good to go. Creeks were the most common places to go fishing back then.

Pollywogging (catfishing at night) was the most fun kind of fishing during that era. We usually went on a Friday or Saturday night after chores around the house were done as a reward for our hard work. One of our favorite places to go was Bassets Creek that runs just east of Chatom past the Hobson Road.

Bobby Lafollette, one of my best friends, usually was invited to go along with Daddy and me. On one particular Saturday afternoon, all three of us left the house for a night of pollywogging. We stopped at Marvin Reed's store in Chatom, and Bobby and I ran in to get all the things we needed for the trip. We had to get liver for bait, and also we had to get snacks such as Cokes, cookies, Vienna sausages, crackers, and even back then, they had rotisserie chicken. We got everything, came sailing out of the store, and jumped in the car heading for the creek.

When we got there, we started making up poles and lines for the drops in the creek. Usually, we made up about a dozen lines and put half up the creek and half down the creek from our camp. All one had to do was tie a string to an overhanging limb or cut a short pole and jab it into the bank as long as the hook and bait were in the water before dark and then build a fire for light and to stay warm if it was cool. Whenever we would check the lines, it was great to see a big ol' mud cat on the end. Sometimes we would catch an eel, and Daddy would toss it back toward Bobby's legs and mine. We would do the Saint Vitus dance to get away from the eel, and then we'd start laughing. On occasion, we would think we would hear a wildcat holler and then be glad to get back to the safety of the fire.

While we were making up the lines on one particular evening, I noticed that Daddy was looking through the bags of supplies Bobby and I had bought. I was standing about twenty feet away from him and was wondering why in the world he was looking from one sack to the other and then back again. I could not figure what he was doing, and then he stopped and looked dead at me.

"Randy," he asked, "where is the liver?" I did a quick scan through my memory from the store: Cokes…check. Chicken…check. Cookies…check. Viennas…check. Liver? Oops!

I could feel the blood leave my face, and I ran through what seemed to be about ten or twelve answers that might save me. I quickly came up with the best one for me, and as calmly as I could, I answered, "I guess Bobby forgot it."

Daddy jumped up, but I couldn't move. He started raising sand and mumbling under his breath as he stormed off up the trail about fifty yards to where the car was parked to drive back to town for the liver. After he left, Bobby scolded me and asked, "Why did you tell him that I forgot it?" I answered, "Because I knew he wouldn't whip you!"

When Daddy returned with the liver, he was laughing about it. We got the lines out, and before long, we were feasting on our snacks.

It turned out to be a good trip, and we caught a mess of pollywogs. I'll bet Bobby doesn't forget the liver the next time we go!

Ol' Bullet Survived, Thankfully for Me

THIS STORY IS ABOUT dogs of earlier times being used more for multitasks than dogs of today—specifically, Ol' Bullet.

Bullet belonged to our neighbors, the Lafollettes, who lived a couple of miles down a dirt road just past our house in Yarbo. It was always fun visiting there because there were more different things to do there than at my house. Bobby Lafollette was one of my best friends. He had a cur dog named Bullet, one of the best hunting dogs ever. Bullet would hunt any kind of game you wanted.

If you were squirrel hunting, Bullet would go tree a squirrel and bark until you got there. The only thing you had to do was stand still and look for the squirrel. He would circle the tree to make the squirrel move around to your side where you could shoot it. At times, Bullet would growl and shake a small bush and sometimes even find a vine that went up the tree. He would catch it in his teeth and pull on it to make the squirrel move or run where you could see it. I have hunted with a lot of so-called squirrel dogs, but none like him. I hunted with one other dog that could do this, but not as well as Bullet.

Bobby and his brother, Willie, had let me hunt with them so many times that Bullet was fairly used to me. There was one happening, however, that nearly changed the history of the friendship with the Lafollettes and me.

I had mentioned to Bobby that I would like to come over and go squirrel hunting with him on this particular Saturday afternoon.

30

Bobby said that they were going to be gone but for me to come over and take Bullet hunting. Not wanting to go by myself, I had asked Daddy to go with me. We drove up to the house that afternoon, and Bullet was sitting on the porch, watching intently as we arrived. We got out with our guns; I whistled for Bullet, but he didn't move. He just sat there like a statue. I called again and still no movement. This caused me to wonder, *What in the world is wrong with him?*

I finally figured out he didn't recognize who was with me, so I sent Daddy in the car to go over on the first hill away from the house and wait for us. Sure enough, as soon as Bullet saw the car disappear over the hill, he quit the porch and ran through the front gate. Bullet and I went through the woods and met Daddy over on the hill. The dog seemed to be okay with everything then. He took off down the branch to look for a squirrel.

In just a few minutes, he had treed one. Daddy and I found the tree and tried to see exactly where Bullet was looking. I was on one side of the tree, and Daddy was to my right. I already had the hammer cocked on my single-barrel shotgun, ready for the squirrel to show himself. Bullet had grabbed a vine, and Daddy was shaking a bush. I guess this was too much excitement for the squirrel; he sailed out of the tree from about forty feet up and dove for the ground. I got him in my sights and decided to shoot him about the time he hit.

At the instant I thought the squirrel was going to hit the ground, I pulled the trigger. I shut my eyes as my 16-guage blasted, and the last thing I looked at was one of the scariest things I had ever seen: Bullet was standing there with his mouth open, the squirrel about to land in it. After I fired, and held that image, I didn't want to open my eyes again. I actually heard Bullet's teeth gnash as he tried to catch the squirrel in his mouth. By some miracle, the pellets had hit the squirrel and missed Bullet.

Heaven forbid what would have happened if I had killed Bullet, the best pet, friend, and hunting dog anyone could want. The friendship between the O'Neals and the Lafollettes may have been broken forever had I ended the dog's life. I guess the good Lord watches over things like this because I have no other explanation of how I missed him.

Needless to say, our hunting trip was cut short. I walked back
to the Lafollette house with Bullet while Daddy trekked back to the
car to come pick me up. I made sure Bullet was back on the porch,
safe and sound, and performed a quick scan over him to make sure he
didn't get even a slight graze from a stray shot. Bullet was fine. I gave
him a quick pat on the head and was so proud that things worked
out the way they did.

I don't think I ever told his owners this story. Did I, Bobby?

Going to Mr. Jim's Field

MR. JIM REYNOLDS, OWNER of the Yarbo store, also owned a small farm about four miles down the Yarbo-Chatom Road. The farm contained several acres that were in cultivation, with corn taking up the largest part of the field. There were several smaller patches of vegetables that had to be maintained from time to time. There were about twenty-or-so head of cattle, and I seem to remember some sheep and goats there also.

The old store was a place where I loved to be whenever I didn't have any chores to do at home. Mr. Jim and his wife, Mrs. Gracie, were raising their grandson, Ralph, who was one of my favorite friends. Ralph was nicknamed Jabo, and some of us called him Jabby. He was a big part of our gang, which meant there were usually several of us hanging around the store.

Mr. Jim had to make several trips from the store to the farm every day to keep check on his livestock mostly and tend to anything else that had to be done with his vegetables. If there were any members of the gang who happened to be hanging around the store, we would all load up onto the back of Mr. Jim's pickup and ride to the farm, just to have something to do. We would gather up a bunch of rocks or raid the bottle caps from the Coke machine and throw them at signs or other friends we would pass along the way. Sometimes we would take sticks and drag them in the dirt while we sat on the tailgate. The old pickup had a very high cattle body on the back. We would climb to the top and let the wind blow in our faces as Mr. Jim drove down the road. He was good to let us have fun like this, but he always told us to be careful and not fall off.

Sometimes there was a bad part about going to the field. There would be times when Mr. Jim would have some chores to do, such as picking beans or peas or shoveling cow manure from the barn to be used as fertilizer. This wasn't fun at all, but we knew that the faster we worked, the quicker we could leave and enjoy the ride back to the store. Back in the day, it was common that if you saw a pickup truck, there was usually somebody riding on the back. People rode on the back of pickups to work, school, church, or going to town to get groceries. I was thinking the other day that I don't remember the last time I saw someone riding in the bed of one. I will tell you now that it was some fun. I hardly ever remember anyone falling off. There was one time, though, that several of us nearly jumped off, but that is another story.

On one of these trips, our friend George (changed to protect myself) went with us. George was always somewhat of a daredevil. He kept a little smirk on his face, as though he had thought of some-thing dangerous to do or get someone else fooled up to do. On the way back to the store, there was a sand bed in the road with ruts deep enough that when another vehicle approached, it had to slow down, but not too slow or it would get stuck in the deep sand. George came up with the bright idea that he could run fifteen miles per hour. As we were approaching the sand bed, he was squatting on the tailgate of the truck and told me to look through the back glass of the cab and tell him when Mr. Jim had slowed down to fifteen registering on the speedometer. When we started into the sand bed, I was watch-ing the speedometer. When we had slowed to twenty mph, I yelled, "Okay!" George bailed off. On his first step, his leg buckled, and his face was the next thing to hit the ground. He then started tumbling head over heels. His arms and legs were outstretched as he twisted and turned. He looked like a rag doll doing cartwheels while sling-ing sand up into the air. He was plowing up more sand than a John Deere tractor could in high gear. We all were lying down laughing in the back of the pickup. As we rounded the curve, the last we saw of Ellis—I mean George—was him slowing down to a roll. After we got to the store, we started walking back to see if he had survived. We went to his house, where he soon showed up walking very slowly up the dirt road. He was all right but was wondering why in the world he was not able to run fifteen miles per hour. I don't think I ever told him any different.

I Want to Go to Graduation, Please!

IT WAS MAY AND time for graduation exercises at the Washington County High School. My brother, Bill, was a graduating senior.

There had been so much talk about it, and I was excited and wanted to go see what all the hoopla was about.

On the day of the big event, I noticed my family getting ready to go, but I hadn't even had a bath. I asked Mama what I was going to wear. I couldn't believe the words coming out of her mouth. It sounded like she said, "You aren't going, young man." I asked her again and received the same reply. At five years old, I couldn't believe she was saying this. "I want to go, Mama!" I kept pleading with, "Mama, Mama, Mama," and then got quiet because I knew after about four "Mamas," I was going to get swatted on the seat of my pants. "No, you're not going," rang in my ears. I began running and crying because I didn't want to stay home with my sisters and miss all the fun.

After a few minutes of crying, I came up with a fantastic idea. I would go and position myself in Daddy's truck and lock the doors so they couldn't go unless I went. I did just that and kind of giggled under my breath and was so proud that I came up with the idea. As it got closer and closer to time to go, I figured they would have missed me by that time and would be looking for me, but they hadn't. I was starting to figure something was wrong with this picture. I was sitting up in the middle of the single-bench Ford and noticed my heart was beginning to beat a little bit faster. I started to think that I couldn't go

36

wearing the dirty shorts and T-shirt I had on. When they did come out and find me, was I going to get a whipping?

Finally, I noticed Mama and Daddy coming out the front door and thought, *This is it! It's coming down to the wire. Something is about to happen for the good, bad or worse.* Then I sat there with an unbelievable look on my face at what I saw: my older brother came driving up in his Ford car, and I sat there and watched as Mama, Daddy, and Bill got in the car and drove off. After about two or three minutes of crying, I figured I at least didn't get a whipping. At that time, I got out, went to my red Radio Flyer wagon, and went riding.

Congratulations to all our graduating seniors in the Washington County schools! And for all the kids out there who didn't get to go to this year's ceremonies, hang in there. You'll get there soon enough.

"Shotgun," I Called It First!

BACK IN THE DAY, we teenagers rode in anything we could find as long as we were going somewhere to do something or get into something. Our parents somehow didn't feel the need to give us transportation unless it was something worthwhile; off goofing around didn't fit into that category to their way of thinking. It was up to us to figure that out. Hitchhiking was the alternative that we used most of the time.

I remember one night Bobby Lafollette came over to Mr. Jim Reynolds's store in his old '56 Ford paper-wood truck. I think at this point in time he didn't even have his driver's license, but his parents trusted him on the dirt road leading from their house and the one mile down the highway to the store. While he was there hanging around with the gang, we kept pestering him and finally talked him into all of us going over to Little Mountain, which was several miles back in woods off the Chatom-Yarbo Road. When he finally agreed, we all bolted to the old truck, several of us hollering, "Shotgun!" For those of you that don't understand what *shotgun* means, it means the seat next to the door on the passenger side. People were being held by the legs, and a couple of shirts were torn while trying to gain this seat. Finally, this seat was captured, and the rest of the gang sat where they could. It was nothing for there to be five or six people in a single-seated pickup, or in this case a paper-wood truck. Now one may think that a driver with this many folks in the cab would be dangerous trying to work the gas, brake, clutch, and floor shift, but our driver was used to this; besides, one of the gang was always trying to give him needed assistance even when he didn't need it. Now that was the least to worry about. There were several of us kids on the back of the truck, hanging onto the paper-wood frame for dear life while Bobby was trying to throw us off by hitting holes in the road and running through mud puddles. The open, rotating dual wheels gave added motivation to the boys riding on the back to maintain the death grip they had on the truck frame. Wow! How much fun could a kid have!

The good Lord was with us once again as we all arrived safely, although the ones on the back had a little more dirt added to their attire. Bobby parked the old truck on a little hill directed back toward the way we came. There was a purpose for parking it like this. The battery in the truck was too weak to turn the engine over to start, so it was positioned to let it roll down the hill, and with the shifter in gear, the driver would let out on the clutch to get the engine to start. Back then, this was a common occurrence because batteries weren't as good as they are today.

We all unloaded and gathered up some fallen limbs to build a fire to provide light. Bobby siphoned some gas from the truck's gas tank for an accelerant, and soon we had a "Babe Jones" fire going. I never knew Mr. Jones, but he must have had a reputation for making huge fires because I have heard this expression all my life. Some of us started wrestling or just goofing off to pass the time. Every now and then, somebody would hoot really loud in an effort to get an owl to answer him. It was quite an accomplishment to get one to answer. When one did answer, everybody had to try it. On occasion, we would holler like a wildcat, just playing crazy. Now y'all get the picture: here are a bunch of kids, miles from home, in an old paper-wood truck that may not start, no flashlight, and get this, no cell phones, and our parents didn't know where we were. All of a sudden, someone said, "Listen, y'all be quiet!" He squalled again. You could have heard a pin drop until…I swear, what seemed like thirty yards away, down the hill in the dark, something squalled back!

We all ran toward the truck hollering, crying and trying to be the first to get inside. No one wanted to be eaten by the wildcat or panther or whatever that thing was. When we heard it squall the second time, we were all inside the truck. And what was so amazing about this? There was no one in the shotgun seat! Now this isn't over yet. Our next major concern was whether or not the truck would start when it rolled down the hill. If it didn't, the next thing to do was for everyone to get out and push, and I don't think there would have been any volunteers. Bobby hollered for everyone to shut up so he could concentrate on what he was doing. The starting of the truck in this manner was indeed not a for-sure thing. If he failed to select the correct gear, the old Ford may not fire off. No one was even breathing as he pushed in the clutch and let the truck gain a little speed off the hill. At what he thought was the right moment, he let out the clutch, and the old V-8 engine fired to life. I'll bet if anyone had been out in their yard at midnight back in Yarbo, they could have heard us hollering and laughing as we knew we were finally headed home.

When we rounded a curve to the left, the windowless passenger door swung open, and we hollered again. I guess we thought the panther had caught up to us and had given it a yank. Let me add this little bit of information here: back in the day, door latches on paper-wood trucks didn't last long for the abuse they took. The redneck way to fix this was to drill a hole through the rain gutter over the door and stick a spike nail or screwdriver down through the hole to keep the door closed. When one got to where he was going, all he had to do was reach up, pull it out, and open the door. Ingenious, huh? I guess we left in such a hurry no one had taken the time to put the screwdriver into the hole.

We rode all the way back to Yarbo with all the boys in the cab of the truck and no one in the shotgun seat. Arriving back at the store, we got out and went to our respective homes. It sure was great to get back to my bed and get safely under the covers. As I drifted off to sleep, I was thinking what an exciting night it had been and chuckled while thinking about the next time we went to Little Mountain, if anyone would want to be riding shotgun.

When Gardening
Was No Hobby

HOME GARDENING THESE DAYS could be called a hobby for some folks as there is somewhat of a pleasure in the smell of fresh-plowed ground in the spring.

There is certainly a feeling of accomplishment when you watch tiny seeds and plants grow into nourishing and delicious vegetables. In earlier times, gardens were a necessity if money was short, and growing your own vegetables was a way to cut down on the grocery bill. Today, we still go to the grocery store and spend more than $200 on groceries and then complain about the high cost. If we were to put back all the prepackaged, microwaveable, further processed food and concentrate on the necessities, our bill would be considerably lower. But I guess I am as guilty as everyone else and do enjoy the convenience and variety of what food stores have to offer.

Daddy's garden was a couple of acres, but we kids called it a field because it seemed quite large when we were required to help work in producing and gathering all those vegetables. I do remember when Daddy thought I was old enough to plow Ol' Dick, our mule. It took all I could do to keep the plow straight and keep from falling down in the flat-broke furrow, all the while trying to talk to Dick to direct him in what I wanted him to do. No, we didn't actually have a conversation during our work, but he did understand a few words; those mostly used were "git up," "whoa," "gee," and "haw." I know that a mule cannot understand many words, but how many of you intellects know the difference between "gee" and "haw"?

Plowing could be somewhat dangerous too. I was small, and one time I got my chin a little too close to the crossbar between the handles while trying to see over it. The plow hit a root and tipped the handles up. The crossbar caught me under the chin, nearly knocking out a couple of teeth; no one had to tell me twice to watch out for that.

The good Lord would usually smile down on us and send adequate rain to ensure the crops grew well. Lush, green gardens were a good sign that plenty of produce would be coming. Although there had already been a great deal of work done, the work was actually just beginning. Picking beans and peas was not one of my favorite things to do; as a matter of fact, I hated it.

I remember I could stay on a hill of butterbeans for what seemed like an hour, moving the leaves around, trying to find all the beans. My older sisters, Peggy and Bonnie, could pick faster than I could, and they didn't mind going on up their row and leaving me behind. It made me smile though, when Mama would get finished with her row and start back on mine to help me. I would then pick at my older sisters when I would get through first.

I remember one time after we had started, Bonnie realized she had come to the bean patch with her good shoes. When she started back to the house to change them, Daddy noticed her leaving. He thought she was quitting, so he got a switch and tore her little legs up. When he looked around at Peggy and me, we started back picking beans and whistling, "She'll be coming 'round the mountain," acting as if we were happy as we could be to be picking.

Picking was one thing, but shelling was another. It was all done by hand, or should I say fingers. It nearly killed me to sit down to a big dishpan full of Miss Irby peas to shell.

Sometimes when I was about halfway through a pan, I would throw an unshelled pea into the hull pile every now and then to help hurry things along. Mother would be suspicious whenever my peas didn't turn out too well. She would dig through the hulls, find them, and I would get the blame.

All the work in the garden and canning was well worth the trouble when we would sit down at the table, say the blessing, and enjoy all the delicious vegetables. And by the way, for those of you who didn't know, "gee" means pull right, and "haw" means pull left.

The Drifter

ON ONE HOT, HUMID day in August of the 1950s, several of us kids were playing out in the front yard in the shade of our huge oak tree. I was playing hopscotch with two of my sisters. We had just eaten lunch and were passing the time away playing in the cool sand.

One of my sisters stopped, pointed, and said "Look, a hobo!" There came a huge old man with a large canvas bag that he could hardly reach around and another as large strapped to his back. We didn't know who he was, so we yelled for Mama, then ran to our front porch. Our house ran only about fifty feet from the highway, so that put him walking fairly close to our house. We weren't saying a word, only watching intently as he was about to walk past. When he got exactly even with our front walk, he stopped, looked dead at us, turned, and walked right into our yard. We were frozen, but Mama had already reached and had the .22 rifle by the door. The old black man set down his bag he was carrying, then slid the straps of the other bag off his shoulders and placed it on the ground. We were dumbstruck and didn't know what to say. Then in a voice and accent we have never heard, he said (speaking to my mom), "Good afternoon, miss. I wonder if you could spare me a glass of water. I've been walking all morning, and I'm might thirsty, if it wouldn't be too much trouble." Mama asked him if he would rather have some iced tea, and he replied, "Yes, ma'am." Mama asked if he was hungry, and he replied, "Yes, ma'am," as his eyes lit up.

Mama returned with the tea and a plate with biscuits, field peas, and collard greens. "You come and sit down on the porch and help yourself," Mama said. "Thank you, ma'am," he replied as he sat on

43

the shaded end of the porch. He didn't say a word as he ate, and we kids had made our way back onto the porch and watched him as he ate. We didn't get close so we could run if he tried to jump us. But he didn't. He finished his meal, thanked Mama again for the lunch, bowed his head, and said, "Lord, bless this house and these children." With that, he donned his huge bags, walked straight out to the highway, turned and looked at us again, gave a nod, and started his slow walk on up the highway toward Millry. We watched as just before he got around the curve of the road, he again stopped, set his bags down on the ground, and sat down on them for a few minutes. He didn't have a hat on, and one could see the sweat on his ebony, bald head glistening in the sun. After a short rest, he again reclaimed his bags and was on his way, out of sight around the curve. That, at this writing, was about sixty years ago. From time to time, I have thought about this old gentleman. Where did he come from as his accent wasn't from around here? Did he have a family? Was he an escapee from some prison? Was he at one time a rich man and had fallen on some bad times? Everyone has a story, and I wonder what his was.

Tale of Embarrassment at the Ol' Swimming Hole

IN MY EARLIER YEARS, the long, hot, humid and lazy days of summer were draining to the soul and body.

During that time, there was hardly any such thing as anyone having a cement pond dug in the backyard.

There was a pool in Chatom, but that was for city folks, and anyway, the lifeguards there wouldn't let you get crazy with your fun, and there were not trees to jump out of.

On any given Saturday morning, Daddy knew that for him to get us to help get something done outside, all he had to do was promise to take us to the Taylor's Creek swim hole at the bridge going to Barlow. All of us would jump in and work our fingers to the bone in great anticipation of "going to the swim hole."

This creek was where I learned to swim. The swim hole had an entrance that was shallow and would gradually get deeper until it got to the "run" of the creek. The sugar-sand bottom felt good to my feet as I would wade out to the deeper part until I was about chin deep and push off the bottom and dog-paddle back to the bank.

I eventually got to where I could do a flip off the 2×10 board that someone had made into a diving board. The creek was cold and deep out in front of the diving board.

This was also a community swim hole, and there would be quite a number of people there on any given Saturday or Sunday summer afternoon.

Churches at this time didn't have baptisteries, so they used creeks or ponds for their baptismal ceremonies. My brother, Bill, related to me a story about a time when he and two of his friends were skinny-dipping at Taylor's Creek. While they were enjoying their swimming, they didn't realize that the congregation from a local church was approaching the swim hole. After realizing they were about to be in real trouble, two ran for safety away from the creek. The other didn't have enough time and resorted to climbing up a tall tree without being noticed and without a single stitch of clothing on his bare body. He got as high as he could in the tree and stayed still, praying he wouldn't be noticed.

After everyone had gathered on the bank, the preacher delivered a small sermon, and the song leader led the congregation in "Shall We Gather at the River." The preacher waded out into the creek and said a few more words, but later, when he raised the head of the woman out of the water, she got a straight-eye shot of a half-hidden, lily-white backside shining between the branches of the tree like the sun reflecting off a mirror.

Then as if she'd seen Jesus himself, the woman went to jumping up and down, pointing toward the heavens and shouting, "Lordy, Jesus! Lordy, Jesus!" The joyous congregation on the creek bank joined in the celebration and began shouting, clapping, jumping up and down, and singing. But the naked boy's nerves wouldn't let him stay in his half-hidden perch any longer. In the commotion, he took his chances and shimmied, slid, and jumped from the tree, snatching his clothes along the way without being seen and before the woman could tell what she had really seen.

He joined the other two boys and ran wide-open back toward home. Once they stopped to rest, he was asked if he thought anybody had recognized him, and he replied, "Not by what they saw, they didn't."

I often pass by the old swimming hole and notice how it has grown up and recall so many good memories of good times shared there with my daddy, family, and other friends. And yes, of the time my brother and his buddies were almost caught skinny-dipping.

Out on the Town

IN MY EARLIER YEARS, my friends and I always looked forward to the weekends and going "out on the town." Out on the town could be in Yarbo or Chatom. At this time, none of the gang had vehicles, so we usually hung out at the old store or hitchhiked a ride to Chatom.

In anticipation of the night, we would clean up and put on some of our best school clothes. Before the night was over, we may have ended up in Chatom or either got into a basketball game in front of the old store and gotten sweaty and dirty; we just kind of played it by ear, so to speak. After several of the gang would show up at the store, we would decide what we were going to do. Sometimes we would just walk the roads that intertwined through old Yarbo and talk to folks sitting on their front porches; we would listen to the radio with them and visit for a while. Then we would venture over to another one of our friend's house and wind up playing cards or checkers. As the night grew on, we would work ourselves back to Mr. Jim's store to get a cold drink and a zoozoo (snack) and just sit out front on one of the benches to see who may be stopping by the store.

If we decided to go to Chatom, we would have to stand out by the road and hitchhike. We didn't have to wait very long and would be glad whenever someone we knew with a fast car would stop to pick us up. We knew who had the fast cars so we would keep up with who we had ridden with and try to get around to riding in all of them. Going to Chatom meant stopping by Joe Thompson's diner (Joe's) to see who all was there and then walk on across town to the show hall. The show hall was a huge building with double doors right in front. There was a large overhang in the front so waiting customers wouldn't have to stand out in the weather before entering. Just inside the doors was this huge popcorn machine that could pop gallons and gallons of popcorn. I can still smell the hot, buttery popcorn as the appetizing aroma met you as you walked in. To make it taste better, we wouldn't buy any when we first entered; we would go all the way down front to watch all the coming attractions, all the while smelling what would be the delicious popcorn. As the main movie would come on, we would go get a big bag of popcorn with a Coke and return to our seats just in time for the movie. Nice! As years passed, we would start working ourselves back up toward the back of the theater to sit. In time, we were all the way in back, making it convenient to see who was sitting in front of us that we could throw ice and popcorn at. When I first started going to the show hall, I do remember thinking this was the first time in my life that I could go out on my own from the house, and here I was, sitting in Chatom with my friends watching a movie; I remember feeling that this was a big change in my growing up.

After the movie, my friends and I would walk back across town to Joe's. We always saved enough money to get a burger, fries, and Coke. We would sit down in one of the many booths and put a quarter in the jukebox selector that was at each table and play a record on the jukebox. As we were eating, we would look around to try to line us up a ride back to Yarbo before everybody left town. It was seven miles to home, and we surely didn't want to walk because there could be wildcats or panthers on the way. One particular time, my cousin, Gene O, had to call his dad to come pick us up. We certainly didn't want to bother him, but we had no choice. He had plenty of words for us when he got there, but after we explained to him that our promised ride had left without us, he was more understanding.

There were times when we had to ride with someone who was reckless and would rather not have been riding with, but we had to get home somehow. If Mr. Jim's store was still open, we would get out there to talk a little more about the night of fun we had experienced. There were more nights that I didn't know if we would get back home in one piece, but by the grace of the good Lord, we always did. Usually Mom and Dad weren't still up when I would come in after midnight, but I imagine Mom was listening for me to come in from "out on the town."

Carjacked

SOMETIMES BACK IN THE '60s, while returning from buying groceries at Reeds Grocery in Chatom, Daddy started noticing something going wrong. The old '49 Chevy had been humming along nicely on our way home. "Oh my goodness," Daddy said so slowly. The rear of the car started moving from side to side, and we knew what it was—A FLAT!

The tire was making a terrible sound as it was flopping about. Daddy pulled over to the side of the road in order to change the tire, but the narrow, uneven shoulder was not one of the best places to stop.

Today, changing a tire is not fun by any means. Probably the hardest thing to do is figure out how to get the tire and jack out of the vehicle. One has to hunt for the driver's manual and try to decipher the illustrations on how to retrieve all the tools for the change; one nearly has to call a high-dollar lawyer for help. Back to my story. The nearly slick spare tire was retrieved from the trunk and placed on the ground out of the way. The jack was found right away, but the foot of the jack was nowhere in sight. Finally, it was located stuck up under some more junk lying in the trunk. The jack, back then, consisted of a three-foot bar with a ratcheting mechanism fastened to it. There was a hook on it also that fit up under the bumper to lift the car as one would jack on the bar. There was one more important part of a jack: the tire tool. The tire tool was a handy-dandy all-purpose tool. There were so many uses of a tire tool other than being used for tire-changing. It could be used as a prying bar as well as a hammer. Ours was well used. We found a piece of wood in the trunk to use

50

to place behind the opposite diagonal tire on the car to keep it from rolling back because the emergency brake didn't hold too well.

It was of utmost importance to place the jack in as straight-up position as possible in order to keep the car from falling over to the side while it was jacked up. After the car was jacked up enough to get some of the weight off the tire, the tire tool (combo lug wrench) was used to loosen the lug nuts. Now do you remember me saying it was sometimes used as a hammer? Daddy was having trouble getting the wrench to fit on the lugs because at some point in time, the wrench was used to beat something that had distorted the end of the wrench. With some expert coaxing, Daddy finally got it on the first lug and removed it, but then he couldn't get it out of the wrench. The lug, while stuck in the wrench, had to be restarted on the stud partially, and then the wrench was removed from it. After this, it would loosen easily with the fingers. Before all the lugs were removed, the car had to be jacked high enough until the tire would clear the ground. Each time the jack would be used to go one higher notch, Daddy would hold his breath that the hook would hold on to the bumper and not jump from under it. I personally witnessed a jack jump out from under the bumper of a car, and the top of the jack dotted the guy right between the eyes. That's something you don't want to see every day. Daddy soon had the spare mounted, and we were on our way home with a slightly distorted bumper. The next day, Daddy made a trip to Chatom to Mr. Buddy Dumas's service station to purchase a new tire. My daddy never owned a new car, but he was very satisfied when he had purchased a brand-new tire to go on the old Chevy. I figure he was counting his blessings. May we count our blessings every day no matter how small.

Close Call with a Chevy

DURING THE TIME MY brother, Roy, was in the Navy, he purchased a '49 Chevrolet sedan for $100 and drove it home from the state of Washington. When he left, he said everyone laughed at him and thought the old car would never make it to Alabama. But he proved them wrong and drove it all the way without the first breakdown.

Our family normally used an old Ford pickup truck that belonged to Woodrow Reynolds Lumber Company. Daddy ran a crew of men and equipment for Woodrow, his nephew, and he would drive the old truck home after work every day. We would use it on weekends to go to the store in Chatom and also to church.

When Roy drove up in the old Chevy and told Daddy he had brought him a car, my daddy was so happy to have a vehicle of our own. My dad owned vehicles before this, but with the old truck to use as he needed, he saw no reason to have a second car because Mama couldn't drive, and he wasn't about to let my brothers take off in our only car.

We thought we were uptown riding in the Chevy. I was about thirteen years old then, and Daddy taught me to drive when he had spare time. I eventually got to take the garbage across the highway and down a dirt road that led to old Yarbo. The trash pile, as we called it, was a place where everyone in the community took their garbage; I would gladly throw the garbage bags in the trunk and haul them off.

When I thought I was far enough from the house that Daddy couldn't see me, I would spin the tires on the dirt and gravel every chance I got. When we would go to church, Daddy would let me drive once we got off the highway and onto the dirt road. Naturally, I couldn't gun it while I had Mama, Daddy, and my sister in the car.

I was about fourteen when I was trusted to drive to the Reynold's store down the road about a quarter of a mile from our house. I loved this because I could go by myself and "hot rod" the old car. The Chevy had a six-cylinder engine and was weak, but I thought it was loaded with power. I would leave the top of the driveway on the hill and give it all it had from there to the store, then slow down just enough to get it stopped as I pulled in. The car had ground-grip tires on the back, and when leaving the store, I would make "U" so the Chevy would be turned up on the side so it could spin and squeal a tire when I hit the pavement. I loved doing this!

But all things don't ever go as planned. I would race down toward the store every time I went, and since the old Chevy didn't have good brakes, I would have to gear the car down. Pulling it down into first gear, I would turn the key off and let the motor bring the car to a stop. I would usually pull up alongside the store and head it toward the woods to keep from hitting anything while trying to stop it. One time, I had pulled off the highway while running about twenty-four mph and was doing pretty good getting the car stopped, but suddenly, I realized some dummy had parked a pickup right smack-dab in the spot where I usually stopped.

I never had a plan B until that moment. The store had a roof that ran from over the front door to the gas pumps that was wide enough so a car could pull up and get gas underneath if it was raining. That was the only path that was available to take. Then came a bigger problem, and it was major! Ms. Gracie, Mr. Jim's wife, who was about sixty-something years old, just happened to be sitting in a chair under the canopy reading the *Mobile Press-Register*. Ms. Gracie was old and couldn't hear too well, and I was processing all this. The Chevy didn't have a horn to blow, and I was hoping and praying she wasn't too engrossed in Ann Landers or a recipe from the Living section so that she could hear me hollering or at least hear the car getting close to her. By the grace of God, she looked up just in time and made one giant leap from the chair to the door of the store. I demolished that chair the instant she vacated it!

After I finally got the car stopped, I got out crying, and Ms. Gracie was crying. But soon we stopped and started laughing. I don't know why unless we were both ecstatic that she was not killed or seriously hurt.

I left the store a bit more sensible that day and never did pull in like that again.

Going Back to Another Time; Only if I Can Take My Air Conditioner

I NOTICED TODAY THE first pleasant, cool breeze and drier air of September, hopefully signaling an early fall to dispel these hot summer days we have been experiencing.

Before long, we will be enjoying cooler nights and nice daytime temps that will prompt more people to get outside and get in some leisurely evening walks and tasks that have been waiting on more comfortable air.

Soon, one will hear rustling leaves falling through the trees and the chatter of squirrels as they play along oak limbs and gather acorns and such for the winter season.

On these cold days to come, it will be toasty warm inside our homes; all we have to do is set the thermostat. This is so convenient, and let me enlighten some of the younger generations about how most of us heated and cooled our houses in the 1950s.

I can remember our house having an electric stove and gas heaters to supplement our fireplaces, but many houses of that era had woodstoves. The woodstove was used for cooking and also served double duty as some heat would drift to other parts of the house. A large woodpile was always kept to serve as fuel for the woodstove and fireplaces.

I guess in previous times, lighter wood (fat wood from pine trees) was mostly used because it would burn at a high temp. We usually used it to start the fires but would use oak wood because it would burn at a lower temp and last longer. Every now and then, one would hear of a house that had burned down because the chimney caught fire from sap buildup that had ignited.

If a fireplace didn't have a fire screen, a piece of hot coal would inevitably pop out of the fireplace onto the floor. When it did, there would be some dancing going on, and the bravest would have to kick it back in. It was common to see burned spots in front of fireplaces as a telltale sign of what had happened.

Insulation was not used in many houses built then. I don't know if it was unavailable or just too expensive to put in. Floors, walls, and ceilings were not insulated, allowing air to seep through the walls into the house. Usually, the air inside was just as hot or cold as it was outside. In the winter, one would have to stand right in front of the fire to get toasty warm. The pants leg would get really hot, and a brother or sister would walk up and pull the pants up against your leg and scorch the hair off it. The chase was on then, but in time, one could return the favor.

We didn't stay cool in the summer. Most folks didn't have air conditioners, so they improvised with both box and oscillating fans. If the room air was hot, the fan would blow hot air across you. The breeze felt good to the sweating skin, though.

In the evening, when the temperature had somewhat subsided, the fans felt pretty darn good. I can remember during the time while I was working in the woods with Daddy that I would have a small box fan blowing on me while I slept. In the morning, before daylight, Daddy would come into my room and turn on the light and turn off the fan. Man! I felt as though I had just lain down to sleep because of being so tired from work the day before. I would lie there trying to wake up, and when I could hear my daddy's footsteps coming again, I would jump straight up and start getting dressed. I didn't want him to call me twice!

I am telling of a time of over fifty years ago. I frequently tell folks that I could go back to that time of "living off the land." But only if I could take my air conditioner with me.

It Can't Get Better Than This

AS TIMES CHANGE, SO does the way we do things in our daily lives that entertain our minds and occupy our leisure time.

There are still kids who are into athletics and other activities that keep their bodies in good shape. And there are those who find that the best way to spend their quality time is by being affixed to their iPhones or computers.

I often think about how back in the early times after the Pony Express, the telegraph was used to send signal impulses through wires to get a message to someone. After the Pony Express, one thought, *It can't get any better than this*, but it did.

The telephone came about, and again, they said the same thing. As time progressed, the telephone made unbelievable strides in technology; first the wireless home phone and now we have the cell phone, which we don't think we can live without.

Texting has now become the choice of communication with friends. Doesn't texting sound and seem so similar to telegraphing? Now again, we can say the same thing, can't we? What can get any better than this?

I remember when we entertained ourselves with whatever we could dream up. Hopscotch, three tin cans, and red rover were the most common things for kids to play. Hard-down tackle football and a baseball game over in the pasture were usually "after dinner on Sunday" sports for everyone to gang up and do.

There was one thing we came up with that was more fun than a barrel of monkeys. It was called a Flying Jenny. Friends, this was loads of fun but at the same time as dangerous as riding a wild bull with yellow jackets after it.

It was a pretty simple setup, as all one had to do was find a tree stump about four feet high or dig a hole and put a sawed-off crosstie in it. Then we'd get a 2 × 10 board about 14 feet long and enter it on the stump, drill a hole in the board, and drive a spike through it, leaving enough room as to not foul the board. Now all you had to do was fasten a handle on each end as you would a seesaw. The only thing different is that on a Flying Jenny, you go around and around instead of up and down.

It took more than two people to operate this thing, however. Kids on each end of the board were the riders, and everyone else did the pushing. It took some muscle for the pushers to get it started because they pushed against the board to keep pressure on it and followed it around to get it moving as fast as they could. After a few rounds, the board would be moving pretty fast, and the pushers had to run to keep up.

For a pusher, there was a major rule to know and heed: if you fell down, you didn't try to stand back up. The other side of the board didn't feel good when it came around and caught you in the back of the head.

When the board was at high speed, it was always fun to see the rider's hair standing straight out behind them. Soon, their color turned a light shade of green as they begged the pushers to stop and let them off. Not on your life! The only way to get off the board was to turn loose and let inertia take its course. It was always funny to see unless it was me.

All right, who's next?

Early Radio and TV Experiences

AS I SAT IN my recliner last evening, I reached for the TV remote that was supposed to be perched on the armrest. But more often than not, it wasn't there, which started an aggravating search for the easily misplaced device. It wasn't beside the cushion or on the windowsill, not in the cubbyhole of my one-year-old granddaughter's favorite riding toy, not in the little pouch on the back of her stroller, and not in the refrigerator or on the bathroom counter. I found it nestled in the newspaper, lying on the floor beside my chair; I wonder how it got there. After going through my favorite channels, I decided to settle on my old standby, Fox News. With virtually an unlimited number of channels, it seemed that you could find one that didn't have the umpteenth rerun on it. There were still some of the same soaps on that had been on for what seemed like an eternity. With the things they could do with face lifts, some of the characters seemed to live on forever (not that I watch them, of course).

I remember when there weren't any TV sets in the neighborhood. Everyone did have radios then, and we listened to our favorite programs of that time. I remember the *Grand Ole Opry* being one that was loved by my parents. Also, there was *The Creaking Door*, a drama/mystery program that, as we listened close in anticipation of what was about the happen, someone would jab us in the ribs and make us jump. *Randy's Record Shop* from Nashville, Tennessee, was another one we loved. During the day, the Big Bam in Montgomery, Alabama, was the most popular station. Saturday mornings were most special to me when I was around five or six as that was the day the *Woody Woodpecker Show* would come on. Mama would finally have to get on to me after it was over because I was walking around mocking the woodpecker yell. I would do the yell for y'all but don't know how to spell it.

The first television I ever saw was at the home of Mr. and Mrs. Romas Carpenter in the Springhill Community. I remember Daddy would take me over there on Friday nights with him to watch boxing. The living room would be full of folks, while others stood on the porch and looked through the windows to watch the fights.

My Uncle Print, who lived across the road from us, finally got a TV. That was very convenient because we could just walk across the road to watch it. Then it wasn't long until we finally got our own black-and-white television. One of the first shows I remember was *Your Hit Parade*, which showcased the latest popular songs of the 1950s. This show lasted fifteen minutes. Other shows were *Water Front, Cannonball, I Married Joan, December Bride, Rin Tin Tin,* and *The Donna Reed Show.* Saturday mornings had *Sky King* and *Jack Jackson, Flying Commando*, and on Sundays, there was *Roy Rogers* and *Dale Evans.* On Sunday evening was my favorite: *Disneyland.* This show made a small child think that there really was a magical land.

As I got older, my two sisters, Peggy and Bonnie, would get me to fill in as a dance partner whenever *American Bandstand* came on. I was very reluctant to do this, but they promised me that if I would dance with them, they would push me in my red wagon when the show was over. They wouldn't always keep their end of the bargain but would convince me to do it again the next evening as well. Some of the favorites on *Bandstand* were Bunny Gibson, Kenny Rossi, Eddie Kelly, Carmen Jimenez, and others we grew to know.

The Mickey Mouse Club also came on every afternoon. This show had many of the Walt Disney characters such as Mickey and Minnie, Pluto, Goofy, Donald Duck, and the rest. On this show also was a series called *The Adventures of Spin and Marty.* This show was about two young men in a Western-style summer camp. They seemed to be always having trouble with each other. I liked Spin but didn't like Marty. My wife tells me she liked Marty but not Spin. Go figure.

I did enjoy all these shows, but mostly I was outside playing ball with my friends or roaming the neighborhood (after all my chores were done, of course). I have so many memories of things that happened while rambling around every day. I would much rather have been doing this than being cooped up in the house watching TV.

Growing up, I would have never believed that programs would change as much as thcy have. I won't get into this as all of you know what I'm talking about. I guess I had better get back to what I was watching. Now what did I do with that remote? It was here a minute ago!

Woodstove Cooking

RECENTLY, SEVERAL OF MY coworkers and I were treated by some sales reps to lunch at the Tokyo Grill and Sushi Bar in Laurel, Mississippi. As I went to wash up, I had this horrible thought: what if we had only chopsticks to use as our eating utensils? I had never had the chance to use them and would have been terribly embarrassed trying to learn in front of everybody. I was relieved to notice on the way back to the table that there were forks on other tables in the dining area. I would hate for them to see me trying to eat rice with my fingers.

It was this ol' mule skinner's first time to sit down to a treat such as this. Nine of us sat down at a semicircle table as this Asian guy started preparing our meal on a rectangular stainless steel cooktop in front of us. He started flipping, slinging, clanging, and juggling a spatula and knife while all the time I was looking for him to make a "mis-lick" and send something sailing my way. He started an egg spinning, picked it up with the spatula, flipped it into the air, and very expertly caught it and flipped it again. He said it was his first day on the job, but this ol' country boy wasn't fooled. The meal consisted of generous portions of rice, shrimp, chicken, steak, vegetables, and noodles. The meal was delicious, and the Asian guy did a great job of entertaining us. I was also reminded of how much things have changed from the old woodstove of earlier times.

When I was a small child, I remember that I definitely was not fond of vegetables; I imagine there are a great many other children that aren't either. I had rather eat meat, not that we had it every meal by any means, and other food such as rice and brown or tomato gravy, mashed potatoes, grits and eggs, and such. My favorite part of a meal was eating syrup and butter with Mama's delicious cat-head biscuits. Mother usually purchased store-bought butter, and sometimes we would get some homemade butter from Ms. Mary Atchison, who had the neighborhood dairy. The thing was to cut a nice dollop of butter, place it in your plate, and pour a good helping of syrup over it, stir it up, and then break off a chunk of a biscuit and drag it through the middle of the mixture. This was so good! I guess I was grown before I discovered that peanut butter tasted so much better to me than the cow butter. This was what I would usu-ally finish up every supper with and would eat it until we were out of biscuits, or I thought that if I were to eat any more, I would pop. Ms. Mary would come weekly and bring fresh milk from her dairy. She made her deliveries in her 1958 four-door Chevrolet. The milk came in glass bottles with a cardboard cap on top. One could see the fresh cream sitting inside the neck of the bottle. Ms. Mary was the classic little old lady with her gray hair rolled up into a nice little bun on top. I stopped by her daughter-in-law's house a few years ago and asked if I could purchase a couple of the bottles if there were any left. I was given three and have them sitting on a shelf with several other of my collectibles as a reminder of that time.

When I was about ten years old, Daddy told me that since a slow rain had set in, he was unable to work in the woods. He said he needed to go see his sister, Donie, and her husband, Hugh Reynolds, to rebuild their back porch, which also covered their water well. This was in the summertime, and school was out, so I went along to assist him by handing him tools or doing other things to help. I was excited about going to visit them because Aunt Donie always spoiled me with treats. Her attire would consist of a long-sleeved, printed cotton dress with a homemade apron with pockets. On the first day we were there, I noticed Aunt Donie opening the door of her woodstove and stoking the coals that were still warm from when she had prepared breakfast. She used short pieces of oakwood that had been split and brought in from the woodpile that was in the backyard. Most every-body back then had woodpiles that supplied the stoves and fireplaces. I could smell the wood burning from the smoke stack that went through the roof of the house. She opened a small door in the top of the stove and pulled out a couple of biscuits, split them open, and placed a few pieces of bacon left over from breakfast between the two halves and brought Daddy and me one each. These were so delicious.

As the stove got hot, Aunt Donie placed a large pot with water on one of the eyes of the stove and, in a little while, filled it with turnip greens. Black skillets, with lard in them, were soon sizzling, and she began frying chicken. At a small table, she got out a large bowl of flour and placed a handful of pure lard in it and started kneading the lard and flower together to make her bread dough. Pinching off a small section of this dough, she would roll it around in her hands, form it into a small flat cake, and place it onto a greased flat pan. She placed the filled pan into a compartment of the stove for baking. The aroma of the smoke from the burning oakwood and the cooking food and bread somehow was so pleasurable that it began fueling my appetite. Daddy had already made a comment that it was working on him too. Finally, after about an hour or so of this enticement, Aunt Donie said, "Y'all go ahead and wash up. Dinner is about ready." She didn't have to tell us twice!

Washing up was accomplished on the back porch next to the well. Water was drawn up from the well by using a rope that ran through a pulley with a bucket hanging on the end. The bucket was let down about twenty feet into the body of water in the bottom of the well until it tilted over and filled up. The bucket of water would be drawn back up and poured into a wash pan that sat on a board about four feet above the floor of the porch. Beside the pan was a saucer with a bar of soap, a mirror on a post, and a towel hanging on a nail. I wasn't tall enough to see in the mirror if my face was clean, so I would just give it a swipe and hope I didn't get sent back for a redo. There was no bathroom in this house, so using the facilities entailed a short walk to the outhouse on the back side of the yard.

When we sat down to eat, we bowed our heads as Uncle Hughey, with his Coke-bottle glasses and Liberty overalls, most humbly said the blessing; I thought he would never get through. On this brightly colored oil tablecloth was a pure feast. There were all the above things mentioned, plus speckled butter beans, field peas, fresh radishes and sliced tomatoes. It was on that very day, which I will remember for the rest of my life that I finally realized how delicious vegetables were. My daddy and I worked there for most of the week, and during that time, we were treated to the likings of fried pork chops, fresh link and patty sausage, bacon (fried and cooked in the vegetables), rice and brown gravy or tomato gravy, fried okra, big lima beans, black-eyed peas, sliced cucumbers in vinegar and black pepper, biscuits, AND corn bread, plus fresh cow's milk and her delicious famous Southern sweet tea. I would observe Aunt Donie, during the day, wearing her faded bonnet to protect her face from the sun, gathering vegetables from the garden. Even though her hands showed signs of many years of work, one could tell the love that was in them as she prepared her meals. It did her heart good to pamper us with her delicious wood-stove cooking while we were there.

Daddy completed the rebuilding of the back porch on about the fourth day. Part of me was glad to finally be done with the task, but part of me was sad, knowing it would probably be a while before my next meal from her old cast-iron woodstove. I will never forget those meals and the daily hugs I got from Aunt Donie.

Barbershops

ABOUT ONCE EVERY FEW weeks, I have to take time out of my busy day to go to the beauty shop for a haircut. In there, one can see all these pictures of lovely ladies with fancy hairdos posted on the walls for a woman to pick out what she would like to look like. The smell of hair spray and other hair chemicals that curl, straighten, and dye ladies' hair fill the air. The skinny little chairs that one sits in to have their haircut are much more suitable for a lady's physique than for a man's. After I take my place in the chair, my favorite hairstylist, Ms. Sharron, gives my hair a few snips with her scissors, and I'm through. Wow! Men's haircuts nowadays are much different from when I was growing up.

My favorite barbershop was in Chatom. It was located behind Reed's Grocery Store, which was very convenient. While my mom was buying groceries, she would send me around the corner to get a fresh haircut. I remember the red-and-white rotating cylinder by the door which all barbershops back then had. The shop was usually busy on Saturdays, which meant I would have to wait a little before my turn. Mr. Dickey and Mr. Murdock were the barbers then, and even though I used both of them, I did have my favorite. I remember sometimes I would pass my turn up to the next person so I could use my favorite. I was a small boy, but I remember some of the men would get a shave before receiving their haircut. The chairs were huge with large padded footrests. The chairs would recline, laying the patron in a horizontal position. The barber would take a piping hot towel and lay it across and around the patron's face and let it soak a little bit before the shave. I was happy that my little peach fuzz didn't require shaving; I don't think I could have stood the hot towel on my tender little cheeks. When the towel was removed, the barber would take a small brush and whip it around a little cup of cream and mop it onto the gentleman's face so that he would look like Santa Claus. A long straight razor would be stroked across a leather strap that was attached to the chair to sharpen. I would watch and hold my breath as the barber would take the razor and scrape the lather and whiskers from the man's face. I just knew any minute that blood was going to fly, but surprisingly, it never did.

It was finally my time. My height was so that the barber would have to jack the chair up so he wouldn't have to stoop over to cut my hair. My barber knew me and my family and would ask how Daddy and Momma and 'em were doing. It took way longer to get my haircut then than it does now, I remember. After he would get through, he would take a small round brush and pour some kind of smell-good powder on it and brush it around my neck. Then he would retrieve a bottle of hair tonic from the shelf and sprinkle it on his hands and run it through my hair, part it and neatly comb it, spin the chair around, and ask for my satisfaction; I never did say that I didn't like it because by this time, I knew my mom was about through, and I was ready to go.

I also traveled to Millry on occasion for a haircut. There was a fabric shop by where Mr. Bowen Caten had his shop. Mr. Caten had a low growling voice that sounded almost like he was gurgling as he talked. He smoked cigarettes, and sometimes the ashes covered more than half the length of the cigarette but somehow wouldn't fall off. I liked Mr. Caten as he talked a lot while he cut hair. I do remember something that happened there that was kind of embarrassing to me. There would be several old men sitting around in the shop telling stories and sometimes colorful jokes. As Mr. Caten was giving me a haircut, one of the old gentlemen told a joke about little Johnny at school. Little Johnny held up his hand for the teacher to recognize him. The teacher noticed him and asked him what he needed. Little Johnny asked something about flatulence. I will stop here with the joke, but Little Johnny's question was so funny that I laughed out loud. Now, friends, this joke was funny, but when it comes a time when you don't need to be laughing, it gets funnier. I was trying to contain my laughing and would try to hold it under my breath. I wasn't laughing out loud but was shaking and could not for the life of me hold still all the while with Mr. Caten trying to finish cutting my hair. Finally, Mr. Caten stopped and said, "Boy, you're gonna have to sit still so I won't gap your hair." I tried and tried but still had trouble trying not to think about the joke. After Mr. Caten had stopped two or three times, I finally contained my hilarity to the point I could sit still, letting him finish his task.

It is amazing how much times have changed, even things as small as going to the barbershop.

Christmases Aren't
What They Used to Be

TECHNOLOGY HAS CHANGED THE toys that kids now get for Christmas. These iPods, iPhone 4, 5, or whatever number they are now seem to be the norm. There doesn't seem to be any limit for what some gifts cost now. I'm sure that these gifts are mostly for teenagers as they feel that they have to stay up with their peers so they can always be in the know of what their friends are doing at each moment of the day. It isn't out of the ordinary for several hundred dollars to be spent on a single gift of this kind. It is true that Barbies, baseballs, and bikes still warm the hearts of so many of the younger boys and girls who haven't had their little world invaded by the social world.

Christmas trees are gotten down from the attic with their pre-strung lighting system, ready to be stood up and turned on; this is very convenient now in our fast-paced world that we live in. I remember when Christmas was a little different compared to today. One of my fondest times was when we would get in Daddy's Ford truck with a newly sharpened axe and venture down an old dirt road in search of the perfect-shaped Christmas tree. Daddy, two of my sisters, and I would walk through the woods until we finally found one that we liked, except it was a little thin on the back side. After walking through several branches and over a few hills, we would come across one that didn't have too many flaws. With a few sharp blows with the axe, the tree was downed. Dragging the tree all the way back to the truck was rough but well worth it when we got it back home and decorated it.

I remember waking up before daylight on Christmas morning and asking Mama if Santa had come already. Daddy would get up and start a fire in the fireplace as we didn't have central heat. I remember getting up and playing with some of the presents in front of the crackling fire. Presents weren't as lavish then as compared to today's gifts. A two-gun holster set, a dump truck, and a football are some of the gifts I remember getting. But I was as proud to get them as I could be. For the record, I never did receive a bike for Christmas. We lived right on Highway 17, and as far as Mama was concerned, it was out of the question for me to get one. I did get a red Radio Flyer wagon once, and I did get more than enough enjoyment out of it. I also stacked lighter and oakwood on it to haul from the woodpile to the scaffold by the chimney. My daddy said it was a good thing that I made good use of it because when he and his brother, Print, were young, they got one once. After a few weeks, they kind of lost interest in it, and it came up missing. The following Christmas, Santa brought them another wagon exactly like the one that came up missing; I wonder how that happened. After that, he said they played with it often all the way into summer. My cousin, Gene O, lived next door to us. He and I got pretty good at figuring out what Santa was bringing us. One Christmas, he was getting some walkie-talkies. We played with those things two weeks at least before Christmas Day came. I know it was hard for him to act surprised whenever he received them on Christmas morning.

Going to Grandma's did not happen for me. The only grandparents I had living when I was small were my maternal grandparents. They lived in Louisiana, so we never made that trip for Christmas because it was too far away. Being the youngest of seven, however, I always enjoyed seeing my older brothers and sisters come back home with their families during the holiday season, especially when they brought me presents.

Let us all remember now that Jesus is the reason for the season. I hope you and yours have a safe and wonderful Christmas and a happy New Year!

Dirt Clods, Bluffs, and Booby Traps

AS I HAVE PREVIOUSLY written, the gang didn't have too many commercial things to play with during our growing-up years in Yarbo, Alabama, so we improvised. Directly across the road from Mr. Jim Reynolds' store was a high bluff that was made when Highway 17 was put through. Over the years after that, the rain and wind caused the steep, sandy dirt to fall off, making deep cuts into the slanted wall of sand. We would dig farther into the voids where the sandy dirt was cool and damp. I know that, at times, we would be back far enough into the bluff that if it were to cave off, someone would have to do some serious digging to get us out. Fortunately for us, that never happened. It did, however, present a good place to have dirt clod wars. In the sand, there were several thousands of small rocks. We boys would gather up a small pile of those balls, hide behind a void in the bluff about twenty feet apart, then start throwing them at one another. It was hilarious when you could hit one of your pals on the backside with one, but a running, screaming child with blood streaming down the side of his head would surely shut down our little war.

There was a trail that was a lower place on the hill that led through the woods over to the Chatom/Yarbo dirt road. This trail was used by families that lived over on that side of the community as they would have to walk to the store because everybody didn't have vehicles then. Beside the trail was a wooden curbed well that had natural spring water coming out from the ground. This spring provided water for families to drink and other household uses. On a hot day, it was refreshing to stop by the spring, lie down on your stomach, and lean over the curb and drink the cool, crystal clear water. Now I know there may be some of you out there that may think that this isn't very sanitary, but let me assure you that it was okay; even the little crawfish in the side of the curb didn't mind.

In season, this hill provided an abundance of violets. Now I'm a guy, the last-born in our family with two older sisters next to me, so I was pulled along with a lot of the things they did. The violets presented a blue/purple mat of flowers across the hill. We would pick as many as we could and give them to my Aunt Alice, neighbors, and my mom.

Mr. Jim and Ms. Gracie Reynolds were raising their grandson, Ralph, better known as Jabo to us. He and I found an old oak tree that had blown down in the branch just north of the store. We climbed on its limbs and kind of turned it into our "fort." There was a trail we had made to the fort, and we thought it would be a good idea to make a booby trap to keep intruders away. We dug a hole in the ground about two feet wide and four feet deep and covered it with small twigs and leaves to hide it.

Next thing to do was to try it out. We finally found another one of the gang from over in Yarbo who had come to the store for a cold drink. We told him we had something to show him, and if he would follow me, we would take him to it. As we approached the trap, I kind of sidestepped around the hole. When I looked back to see if he was going to fall in, I noticed Jabo had his hand on the side of his shoulder to help guide him to our intended destination for him. At about the same time, I could see our friend's eyes roll up into his head as his feet left firm ground and, slick as a whistle, disappear into the hole. He was hollering, then screaming something that sounded like "Help!" while Jabo and I were rolling on the ground laughing.

Climbing out of the hole, he was spitting and sputtering, trying to get the dirt out of his eyes and mouth, which made us laugh even harder. Soon though, he was laughing too. In order to make up to him for the dirty trick we had pulled on him, we suggested that he go find someone else who might want to see our fort. Jabo warned, "Just make sure they're not bigger than we are or can outrun us!"

Long Trails

MY TWO SISTERS NEXT to me, Peggy and Bonnie, and I would often walk through the trails behind our house to where the Lafollette kids lived. It was a long walk, about two miles, to their house. We would sometimes go when, by chance, it would happen to be about lunchtime. Ms. Edna was a great cook, and vegetables somehow tasted better at her house. We would have fun playing and running around the surrounding woods. There was a swing that was attached to a huge oak limb that was about thirty feet off the ground. Someone would get in the swing to get it started. Another person would push them from behind and run all the way under them, which would make them go pretty high. If someone wanted to show out, they would go high and sail out of the swing to see how far they could go before landing in the sand. Usually, there would be two funny things that would happen before the day was out: one was someone would fall out and get the breath knocked out of them, and the other was somebody would land wrong and bite their lip or tongue. It was hard to see where the bleeding was coming from with a mouth full of sand. Fun times indeed.

Throwing knives at tree trunks to see how far away one could stand and make it stick was always a challenge. One thing no one wanted to do was stand too close to the tree because a buzzing knife reeling off its mark from the tree, I admit, was a little dangerous. Ms. Edna was good to let us do these things as long as we were careful, but if she couldn't see us, then what difference did it matter?

One day after playing for several hours, my two sisters and I started on our trek back to our house. About halfway back, I saw that

I was getting the urge to go, and it wasn't a quick go. It was about six o'clock in the afternoon at the time, and there was always talk of wildcats in these woods. I pleaded for my sisters to wait because of the pain mounting in my belly, and I was seeing that I was about to get to a decision-making time. I was lagging behind and listening to my sisters giggling, which didn't help my feelings at all. I didn't want to start laughing too as that made it harder to concentrate on my task at hand. Beads of sweat were breaking out on me. I was beginning to see that they had the "every man for himself" attitude. I thought my sisters loved me, but I was beginning to wonder. You know, friends, there are little happenings in life that happen that one never forgets, and I was figuring this was going to be one of those times. After several hundred yards of pleading and crying and promising to help do their part of their chores, my time was running out; I was either going to stop and do what I had to do and get left for the wildcats to eat or let nature take its course. Now I don't want to get too descriptive about my decision, but they didn't wait, and I didn't get eaten by a wildcat. The only hint I will give my readers is that my sisters wouldn't let me get any closer than fifteen feet of them on the rest of our walk. Y'all have a good day and always watch out for those wildcats!

Ice Cream the Hard Way

THE FOURTH OF JULY is a time that we all look forward to. It is a time when family and friends gather to celebrate with good food and, sometimes, fireworks. Barbecues, with all the potato salads, baked beans, corn on the cob, and watermelon are probably the most common menu across the land. I imagine so many people don't realize what the true meaning of the Fourth is all about. It is a celebration of the complete separation from the rule of Great Britain. On July 4, 1776, the Declaration of Independence was adopted. The Declaration of Independence proclaimed liberty throughout the land and to all the inhabitants thereof.

Probably one of the best things people look forward to on the Fourth is homemade ice cream. Making it is pretty easy. With an electric ice cream maker, one just purchases some ready-to-use ice cream mix, pour it in the cylinder, fill the sides with ice and ice cream salt, cover the maker with a heavy cloth, plug it up, and let her run while you sit inside in seventy-degree air conditioning. When the motor starts pulling down, you know the cream is about ready. An addition of peaches or strawberries into the mix beforehand makes it all the more enjoyable.

I was recently talking to an acquaintance of mine, Ms. Pearl Gant, of the Aquilla community. She and I were talking about the making of ice cream, and she shared with me about how it was when she was a little girl. She said that refrigerators weren't that common during that time. On July 3, her dad would purchase a three-hundred-pound block of ice from the ice house. He would have already dug a deep hole in the ground that would accommodate the huge block of ice. They would wrap the ice in a quilt, lower it into the ground, and then insulate it with sawdust around the sides until ready for use. Ice was then chipped from the block and used around the sides of the canister of the maker. Her mother would prepare a special recipe mixture of the cream that had been handed down from generations before. The top of the maker was a gear with a hand crank on the side for the men to turn. A quilt would be folded and placed on the top to help insulate the freezing mixture. Kids would take turns sitting on top while the machine was cranked. When the ice cream was ready, the dasher would be pulled, and any ice cream on it was given to the kids.

Ms. Gant also remembered when about seven or eight, kids would ride the school bus driven by Mr. AD Britton. Mr. Britton would let them know on what day he would stop by Mr. Otto Dearmon's store in Healing Springs. The kids would save their money and have it ready to go inside the store and get a double-dip cone for 5 cents. She says she can still remember that time and how special it was to look forward to this delicacy.

I'll bet she was thinking, *It can't get any better than this*, but yet it has. Time never stands still, and things are always changing. I think I'll go to the store and pick up my favorite—Neapolitan.

Old time recipe: 6 eggs well beaten, 2 cups sugar, 1 can Eagle brand milk, 1 small can Pet milk, 1 carton half and half, additional milk to fill 1 gal freezer, 1 tsp vanilla. Enjoy!

Play Ball!

A FEW WEEKS AGO, I pulled over by the side of the roadway on Highway 17 north of Chatom. I got out of my car and stood for a few moments and listened to the relaxing sound of the gentle breeze as it blew through the nearly grown pine trees. This was a place that was, at one time, often filled with people enjoying playing ball. I could almost hear the umpire yell, "Play ball!" and hear the crack of the bat as it came in contact with a baseball or softball. I was standing at what used to be named the Yarbo Ball Diamond.

On any given Saturday or Sunday afternoon, dozens of avid ballplayers and spectators gathered here as a break from work or school. Lights were eventually erected to facilitate nighttime playing which, on tournament nights, would go on until way after midnight. I remember ladies' softball teams from surrounding areas would come and participate in tournaments. Ladies' teams from Millry (sponsored by Barbers Milk), Red Creek (the Sweethearts), Wagarville Women, Baxter's Bombers, Kellers, Sonny's Honeys, and a team that was coached by the well-known Bert Hankins (sponsored by Onderdonk QH, then changed to Hankins Cattle, and finally the Blue Angels). Other teams were the Lady Warriors and the Crickets from Mount Vernon.

Games weren't without interruptions after an important call had been made by the umpire. I remember one umpire who would make a call, and no one would argue with him; his name was Mr. Delbert Carney. Mr. Carney knew the game, and when he made a call, that was it! Sometimes spectators would argue about a call, and I do remember some of them would get into fisticuffs over it. There was one time when an argument started in the stands and wound up behind the bleachers in the grass. I don't remember the names, but there was some hairpulling involved.

A friend of mine says he remembers Lamar Carpenter, who was playing center field, yelling, "Get out of HERE!" after a hard-hit ball passed over his head, fence, and into the tall pine trees that lined the outfield fence.

Parking was sparse, so the sides of Highway 17 were lined with numerous vehicles on either side. Children ran about playing chase and hide-and-go-seek among them. Whenever a passing car would squall its tires in braking, mothers would run frantically while holding their breath until they found that their kids were safe.

There was no water available at the Yarbo ball diamond. If one didn't bring his own water, there was a trail behind the field that led to a small stream of water about a hundred yards away. If he was thirsty enough, it didn't matter about getting down on his stomach and drinking from the cool stream. It may have been unsafe, but I have drunk from this stream plenty of times to quench my thirst.

I know there are plenty of readers out there that could share lots of their own stories about this ball field. Now only the ones that enjoyed this place remember all the fun that was experienced here. The sounds of people enjoying one of America's favorite sports have been silenced here and replaced by an occasional passing car and the gentle breeze as it passes through the beautiful pines.

Unique Fishing Bait

SUMMER HAS NEARLY PASSED, and some of the last fishing days for the casual fisherman are left. Recently, while cutting one of my customer's yards, I spied some of those little black grasshoppers with the definitive orange down their backs, and it reminded me of a fishing trip that happened thirty-something years ago. My son, Brady, who at the time was about five years old, was asking me about taking him fishing. Since we lived on the Emmett Wood Lake Road in Millry, a fishing trip was not much of a problem. I relented after about fifty of the "Can we, Dad, please, please." As I was getting the poles together, I noticed Brady had disappeared. I was loading the poles onto the back of the pickup when he returned with a Maxwell House coffee can with a couple of dozen of those little black grass-hoppers described above. I asked him what he was going to do with them, and he replied, "We can use them for bait." After taking the coffee can from him and slinging the little insects across the yard, I told my son that we wouldn't be able to catch anything with those things. I don't know what he said, but he was mumbling something kind of under his breath.

Arriving at the lake's office, there were two men just pulling up to weigh their catch. Brady and I looked in amazement at the nice long stringer of huge bream they pulled from the back of their truck. Wow, that was a nice catch, which made us more anxious to get our hooks in the water. After talking to them for just a second, I asked the wrong question: "What did y'all use for bait?" The answer they gave didn't sit very well with my little man. One of the gentleman said, "You know those little black grasshoppers with the orange stripe down their back?" About that time, I felt my son's hand slap the seat of my pants, and he looked up at me and said, "Dad!" I looked down at him, and I cannot describe the look on his little face. It was a mixture of disappointment, sadness, and two or three other things. I can't describe the look on my face either, but I felt pretty stupid. Brady immediately turned on his heels and told me, "Come on. We can still catch them."

After a quick trip back to the house, we found most of the creatures were still close to where I had set them free from the coffee can, and I was sure there helping Brady to recapture what we could. We couldn't get back to the lake quickly enough to get those things in the water. We didn't catch as many bream as those two guys did, but we were proud of the nice ones we caught for supper. My son and wife shared that little tale of a fishing trip with many people for a long time, and I am reminded by them pretty frequently about how much I know about fish bait. So this summer, if you find those little black grasshoppers with the definitive bright-orange stripes down their backs, they sure will give you a good chance of bringing back a nice mess of fish for supper.

Ax Men

I SIT HERE IN amazement as I watch the show *Ax Men* on TV. With the equipment now costing thousands and thousands of dollars, I am reminded of how simple my dad's operation was. We would haul about five cords of wood to the wood yard each day, adding up to about twenty-five cords a week, which would be nothing compared to the operations of today.

Our basic ways of cutting wood when I was growing up was a Homelite chain saw and a couple of axes. When I first started using an axe, my daddy said, "Boy, you had better put some gloves on those tender hands before you start with that axe." I replied, "Naw, Daddy, I don't need 'em." Well, that was another one of those times I should have listened to him. Within a couple of hours, I had worked up several water blisters in each hand. I didn't want to tell him, but when he saw me sneaking a pair of cotton gloves from the old Ford paper-wood truck, he had to say, "Just wouldn't listen, would you?"

I became quite the axman. If I wasn't skidding logs with our mule, I was using the blade of the axe resting on the heel of my boot on a slant to sharpen it. A brand-new flat file with a corncob on the end for a handle was used to sharpen the axe. Every stroke of the file across the blade to the end of the blade would leave a nice streak of new metal exposed. Working the streaks across the blade to the end of the blade on both sides would leave a nice sharp blade. A good way to test the sharpness was to see if it would shave the hair off your arm without cutting yourself, of course. The sharper the axe, the fewer blows it took to chop the limbs of the pine trees off after they were downed. One had to be very careful when using an axe. It was important to cut where you were looking; a missed blow could deflect the axe, and that would be a good way to get the nickname peg leg.

At home, an axe was also used to split firewood if the chunks were too big to put into the fireplace. I don't think I ever did see a wood-splitter until I was a grown man; we couldn't have afforded one anyway. Splitting wood with an axe also took some skill. If you didn't know how, it was very easy to sink the axe deep into the wood and get it stuck. I did this once and broke the handle trying to get it out. Daddy threatened to hold the price of handle out of my paycheck. Fortunately, he didn't because I wouldn't have made much that week if he had. My dad taught me to aim a couple of inches from the edge of the wood and just before the axe hit the end of the piece of wood to twist my wrist just a little. This would make a piece of wood fly off the block of wood being split and cut flips across the ground. I got so good at this that I could actually make the wood stack itself as I cut them off...well, almost.

My dad always had an answer for everything, but sometimes his answers I kind of questioned. I asked him once why some axes had two blades; his answer was, "So you can chop in front of as well as behind yourself"?

Barlows and Pocket Holes

I RECENTLY ASKED MY ten-year-old grandson to show me what all he had in his pockets, just to see the difference in what boys carried now as to when I was growing up. They were empty, but he was disgruntled because he had misplaced his new Case knife. I was disappointed that he had misplaced it but was glad to hear that he did regularly carry a pocketknife, except to school, of course.

I do remember as I was growing up the knife of choice was the old dependable "Barlow." My Barlow sported two blades, one about three inches and another about two inches long. I had to do a lot of sharpening to keep them relatively sharp. I used it to whittle, cut down small bushes, and throw at targets such as trees or a cardboard box. The long blade was used to clean one's fingernails also, not that mine were ever dirty. Occasionally I would use it to mark out a circle for a quick game of marbles. My buddies and I would sometimes play "Mumbly Peg." The long blade of the Barlow would be fully extended, and the shorter blade would be only halfway open. First, stick the short blade in the ground and then place your finger at the base of the knife, flip it up into the air and try to get the longer blade to stick into the ground for two points. If it landed and stuck any other way, then it would be only one point. If it landed on its side, then that player would lose his turn. The objective of the game was to see who could get to twenty-one points first.

Marbles were carried in my pockets in case I would run across someone who wanted to have a quick game of marbles. It would be customary to have at least one heavy "log roller" marble that was heavy enough to knock your opponents out of the circle. In marbles, the winner would keep ever how many of his rival's marbles he could knock out. Sometimes I would leave a game with most pockets full of marbles, but there were times when I lost all my marbles. Every now and then today, I feel like I have lost all my marbles!

I would also carry a rabbit's foot for good luck even though sometimes I didn't think it helped much. It would be attached to a piece of metal and would have a little chain loop around that.

I don't remember getting a salary but would usually have some change in my pocket from doing extra chores around the house or for some of my neighbors. In the '50s, whenever one would buy a bottle of soda, a deposit was charged for the bottle, which was an extra two or three cents. With this in mind, I would scour the neighborhood and beside the highway looking for bottles. A case of twenty-four empty bottles would put a little jingle in my pocket. That wasn't much, but for a quarter, I could get a king-size Coke and a banana flip, which was one of my favorite treats at Mr. Jim Reynolds' store in Yarbo.

Bottle caps collected from the Coke box at the store or found around the store yard were other items that could be found in boys' pockets. They were used to throw at my pals or at different obstacles.

With all these things carried in my pockets, it wasn't too uncommon to have a hole occur in the bottom of it. The hole wasn't very noticeable until I would notice something from my pocket rolling down my leg. At that time, I would have to get my mom to sew it up whenever she would have time.

Maybe I need to ask my grandson to check to see if he has "a hole in his pocket"!

Our Neighbor's Mule and Daddy's Truck

BEING RAISED IN THE country back in the 1950s and 1960s was quite an experience. I was raised on a farm with about four acres under cultivation. We used a mule and plows as purchasing a tractor was for rich folks. We didn't have to spend any money for gas and upkeep on a mule. On this particular Saturday, we had quite a bit of plowing to do. Our mule, Dick, wasn't feeling too well, so Daddy and I went over to Mr. Ferguson's to borrow his mule, Ada.

Daddy drove an old '52 model Ford pickup with a board frame on the back body and a tarpaulin stretched tight and tacked down around the edge. The old truck had no mirrors on the side or in the cab to see out of the back. Daddy suggested that I climb over inside the back of the truck, take the reins, and lead Ada back to the house that way. Well, I was a little skeptical of this, but I certainly didn't want to ride Ada bareback, so I did as he asked (I never did talk back to Daddy). As I was climbing over in the back, I told Daddy, "Don't go too fast." I don't think he heard me.

When we left, ol' Ada kind of trotted along behind the pickup without too much of a problem. After we were about a quarter of a mile into the journey, I noticed Daddy had somehow sped up just a little bit, and Ada was having to break from a trot into a run every now and then to stay caught up. Before long, Ada was pulling on the reins a little as if to say that she didn't like this too much. I hollered at Daddy to slow down some, but because the old truck didn't have a muffler, he couldn't hear me. Then I sensed that we were still gaining a little speed, and poor Ada was moving her little legs as fast as she could, breaking from trot into a gallop. I noticed that one of the chains had come loose and was flying around under her legs, scaring her.

About this time, I was getting a sense of a dangerous situation. Ada was pulling back as hard as she could against the reins, and I had to double-wrap my hands around them so she wouldn't tear loose. If she had broken free, we would have never caught her, and the next thing would have been me getting my tail torn up for letting her go.

By this time, I was screaming and crying for Daddy to slow down, but evidently, he had his mind on getting home and getting to work. In order to keep myself from being dragged out of the pickup bed by the mule, I put both feet against the tailgate and had the reins wrapped around both hands while trying to hold on. As Ada pulled hard against the reins, I could feel my behind come off the floor of the truck. I could clearly see that I was going to get pulled out of the truck. I suddenly realized that I was about to make the decision to let her go or get pulled out. Now, folks, I'm a believer, and I know that just before I got dragged out of the truck, the good Lord must have reached down and given Ada a little shove to help her and save me. Thank you, Jesus!

We soon got to the highway crossing and had to stop. We pulled across the highway, home at last. Somehow, we had all arrived safely. Ada was standing there all lathered up and trying to catch her breath, and I was wiping tears. Daddy said, "That worked pretty good, didn't it?" I just looked at Ada and whispered, "Sure glad we didn't come back by the highway."

My Adventures as a Mule Skinner

BY THE TIME I was twelve or thirteen, I had to go to work with my daddy in the paper woods, as did my older brothers when they were growing up. This was extremely hard work to say the least. The first day on the job, we were cutting wood just east of Millry around the Mount Carmel community, and the woods there were so thick that you couldn't cut a tree down that would fall all the way to the ground.

My distinguished job was mule skinner. Our old mule, Dick, and I would have to tong the butt of the tree and pull it to the ground to be cut in order for Dick and me to take it to the landing before being loaded onto our truck. The wood would be cut into five-foot, three-inch lengths. After this, one man could shoulder the wood and stack it onto the back of the truck.

There was this one huge stick of wood that probably weighed over two hundred pounds. I volunteered to carry it and had to help my friend Bobby pick up one end. Daddy was on top of the half-loaded truck with a pick to help us after we got the end of it up to the stack. The wood was so heavy that I couldn't breathe, and when I turned my back to the truck for Bobby to help me give a boost, my daddy said (and I am paraphrasing,) "Break wind and jerk high." I immediately lost pressure and tried to get out from under the piece of wood without it killing me. We all laughed for a while and then tried it again. About the time we started to boost it, Daddy said, "I'm not gonna say anything," and we lost it again. It took several more attempts before we finally got it on the truck without getting hurt.

If I wasn't in school, I worked with him in the woods until I was eighteen. I always enjoyed the people that worked with us in the woods—Bobby Lafollette, Les Franks, and Bobby White—as well as many more who are still my friends today. I will see one of them in town and say, "Let's go jump a load," and they will say "All right, let's go!"

By general rule, we would get two loads of wood a day. Daddy always thought we could do more, so one day, we decided we would do it for him. We got started right after daybreak and sent the first load out in good time. Daddy was soon back, and we got the second load out a little after dinnertime. We were getting pretty tired by this time and sat down for a well-deserved lunch of sandwiches, Viennas, pork and beans, and such and then took a rest.

About two o'clock, Daddy was back, and we didn't have too good of a start on the elusive load number 3. We loaded the wood we had ready and set out to cut the rest. About this time, the chain on the saw broke, and it took a little while to get it fixed. I could see Daddy was getting a little anxious as our time was running out to get to the wood yard before four o'clock. The old Ford truck then wouldn't start, and we had to go to the top of the hill to finish loading it. Daddy had to work about an hour, and the clock was still ticking. When he finally fixed it and we got loaded, I noticed that it was exactly four o'clock. Daddy was aggravated then, and if we didn't get the last load delivered, it meant we would have to wait until the next morning for the yard to open. He was aggravated and hungry, and we were staying out of the way.

When he started to bind the logs down, the chain wasn't quite tight enough, and he opened the binders to catch one more length. When he gave a big heave on the binder, it was just too much for the old chain, and it broke! Daddy then leaned his head against the load of wood and started saying his Sunday school lesson backward. That was the last day he asked us to get three loads of wood.

The Juke

THE MUSIC WAS VERY loud but still somehow pleasant to listen to as the bass beat was reverberating throughout the neighborhood. The jukebox was playing some '50s songs while fun was being enjoyed inside the swaggered roof of the paint-peeling, clapboard building. Steel bars decorated the windows as a protection from after-hour break-ins, I guess. A single gas pump sat in front of the overhung roof that protruded from the building. Inside, guys and gals enjoyed the merriment of dancing and someone trying to sing louder than the jukebox was blaring.

This was a typical 1950s Saturday night happening at the juke in Yarbo, Alabama, better known as the Sunset Inn. This establishment was about fifty yards from where I was raised, and it belonged to my uncle. One had to pass through a screen door, which had a push-bar with a Sunbeam Bread advertisement on it, which also had a picture of a little girl holding a piece of light bread. Inside the floor was of a smooth, worn 1 × 4 board pine floor that showed years of wear. There were about eight four-foot square wooden tables with a couple that were longer. The chairs were silver and red with bright-silver buttons on the backs. About twenty feet from the front door, there was about a fifteen-foot bar that had wooden stools sitting in front for the patrons. There was a lattice wall that separated the dining area from the dance floor. This room was where the jukebox was located. I remember well, after sixty some-odd years, on the back wall of the dance room was some kind of cola advertisement, about two and a half feet tall by six feet wide, that had the most beautiful woman, maybe Loretta Young, in a long white evening dress, reclining on a daybed holding a bottle of cola.

There were several more small rooms in the back, but I don't know what they were for. In the very back was a larger room which held some more tables, and I believe that was where card games and some dice-rolling went on. In the wintertime, there would be some fires outside where partygoers could gather around for warmth while they enjoyed their alcohol and visiting. Yarbo had a large sawmill with the town built around it which provided work for people to provide for their families. Yarbo was one of the larger towns around, and the juke was a place to go to party after a long hard workweek. At one time, there were three jukes within a few hundred yards of each other. People from different walks of life would go to the juke that best suited their interests. My dad ran one and would order fish from Mobile to come up on the Doodle-bug on Fridays. The Doodle-bug was a single car that ran the rails and carried passengers and a little freight. When the fish were cooked, my dad added some strong seasoning and a little hot sauce to make it more appetizing. With the added seasoning, the selling of colas went up dramatically. Barbecue chicken and pork were also added to the menu. With all this food, drink, music, and gambling supplied, there were many Monday mornings when plenty of workers would show up for work with all their previous week's earnings gone.

The juke was a place to go to have fun, drink, eat, gamble, and have whatever kind of fun patrons wanted to have. One of my brothers remembers that when he was a boy, he was sitting on the bar with his back leaned up against the wall. All of a sudden, a bullet came through the wall, which was a little too close for comfort; time to go home! Yes, there were times when someone would have a little too much to drink, have a little too much fun, and get into somebody else's way or say something with their mouth that their rear end couldn't back up, then trouble would happen. I have heard several tales but can't go into it because I wasn't there. At times my uncle would have to have my dad back him up in some instances because things got pretty rough. I have heard tales of bullets skipping fire down the blacktop while somebody was shooting at somebody running away from trouble they had started. When my dad was running the juke, there was one occasion when a big argument broke out between two of the patrons. Some kind of fight ensued, and one of the patrons met their demise that night.

On one hot summer night, we were all sitting on our front porch. Someone noticed there was a sound that was kind of similar to a heartbeat coming from over in the woods across from our house. This was something we had never heard before and was very eerie. My dad and two of my brothers took their shotguns and went to investigate the sound. The rest of us went inside the house because we were frightened and didn't want whatever it was to come get us. After about thirty minutes, they came back from down the direction of old Yarbo. They were trying to be serious and tell us it was a big monster that they had to shoot. One of my brothers started laughing, which was a telltale sign that the story wasn't the truth. Daddy finally said that they did find the origin of the eerie sound. It was the bass from the jukebox at Sandbed Joe's Juke, which was in old Yarbo. We were all deeply relieved that the sound was identified.

A few years after the war ended, the Ingram-Day sawmill shut down, and the jukes seemed to disappear. Sunset Inn was shut down in Yarbo and established again in Citronelle; this was called Sunset Inn No. 2, and there was also a No. 3 to follow. I'm sure there are several people around who, at some time or another, visited and enjoyed the juke. I'm also sure they have lots of tales to tell of times they had there and survived, or maybe they will choose to keep those experiences to themselves.

Friends

"FRIENDS" CAN CARRY A wide range of definitions. There are friends who are just acquaintances that we see from time to time. They can be people that we enjoy being around and see from time to time and spend a little time with. There are also friends that we spend a great deal of time with and just enjoy their company. Then there are friends who fall into the category of being special friends that we share things with and get along with well enough to be called lifelong friends. Friends like this are friends that almost nothing can tear their friendship apart—well, almost nothing. I know of two guys that fall into this definition.

These two guys were born only a few miles from each other. They went to church and school and played together when they were small. In high school, they played football together for several years. In time, they joined the Navy at the same time and still remain the best of friends. At this time, I will just say they are in their "very" senior years. These two guys are my brother, Tommy O'Neal, and his friend, Dalco Beech.

As I said, their friendship has been lifelong, and both have raised beautiful families. I also said there was "nearly" nothing that could break up their friendship. That "nearly" happened just after they got out of high school. In the early fifties, they both had found jobs but at different places. In a short time, they each had purchased an old car and were enjoying them. At some point in time, Dalco's car had broken down and was undriveable. On this weekend, Tommy was working, so Dalco had asked Tommy if he could borrow his car since he had to work. Now friends are friends, but loaning your buddy your car to go and do as he wished was a little stretch, but being the persistent person Dalco was, he talked Tommy into it. Dalco assured him he would take extra good care of his car. Tommy's car was a 1931 T-Model Ford that he had purchased for seventy-five dollars from Tommy Dyass Motor Company in Chatom. The car was a four-door that was fairly nice with all the roll-up windows in good working order. The seats were nice, and the car was in all around pretty good shape. All this took place around 1950.

Somehow, and only the ones who know Dalco can under-stand what happened next. Dalco was sitting on his porch looking at Tommy's car and came up with the idea that there was something he could do to make the car more beautiful, appealing, or whatever he was thinking in his head. Why he thought he could do this with-out even checking with Tommy first was unimaginable, but being the friends he figured they were, he thought Tommy would readily approve. Dalco, on his own accord, proceeded with his plan to make the T-Model beautiful and more appealing.

On Monday morning, Dalco (I know it had to be reluctantly) brought Tommy his car back. When my brother walked out on the front porch and saw what he saw, he went silent. Tommy walked out and slowly walked around the car without saying a word. Then after a few minutes of silence, he said, "Dalco, you have ruined my car!"

I know Dalco was as silent as Tommy was during those long few minutes and was holding his breath while waiting on Tommy's reaction to what he had done. When Dalco left with Tommy's car, it was a four-door full-metal rooftop car. When he brought it back, it was a convertible. The only thing was it wasn't a ragtop or anything! Dalco had taken a hammer and a cold chisel and proceeded to cut the complete metal top off and throw it away! He also had removed the four doors and discarded those. He had taken some bailing wire and wired the fenders to the frame to keep them from rubbing the tires. Then he had taken some boards and used those to replace the nice seats. Tommy finally said, "I like it!" After this, Dalco was grin-ning like a mule eating briars. They drove this thing to all the local swim holes and even to the new large swimming pool in Jackson. I have heard lots of stories about this strip-down, and I know they enjoyed this new modified ride for years to come. I remember sitting in it and playing when I was a small boy, imagining myself driving it down the road and having fun.

So this story is about the true friendship my brother Tommy and Dalco have shared over the years, and it still continues until this day. However, Tommy never loaned Dalco any car after that. It has been, as I have said, a lifelong friendship.

Tall Tales from Table 8

ALMOST EVERY SMALL TOWN has one of these. It is usually a little place that is, in plain view, a daily gathering place where a few folks from every walk of life come to have breakfast or just a cup of coffee and catch up on the overnight news before starting their day. It's a place to meet old friends that we look forward to seeing and spend a few minutes together. I tell my wife it's my *Cheers*, which was a television show about a local bar where everybody went to relax and have a beer. Our place, in the small town of Chatom, Alabama, where I live, is called Jake's.

Table 8 is a round table with a lazy Susan, six feet in diameter, and sits right up next to the waitresses' bar. Table 8 has already gotten a name for itself as being where some of the local town rumors are started. One must have pre-applied before getting to sit at this table. All the regulars have their seats, and the ones who have been there the longest have seniority. That means his other buddies will quickly tell anyone who unknowingly tries to sit down in that seat that it is saved for the regular who is about due to arrive. Some arrive early and stay the duration of the morning while others watch the clock on the wall and stay as long as they can and still make their "get to work time" at their respective jobs. We have lawyers, engineers, probate judges, loggers, mechanics, hunters, fishermen, doctors, car salesmen, chicken doctors, retirees, business owners, horse traders, newsmen, teachers, and preachers. We also have hunters that think they are fishermen, mechanics that think they are probate judges, retirees who think they are engineers, businessmen who think they are doctors, and…you get the picture. The waitresses know all of us and our special little quirks.

They know who likes their coffee in small cups as well as those who love huge cups. They can see someone walk in the door and automatically holler at the cooks in the kitchen what to start cooking.

The walls are adorned with relics and antiques. One of the walls also is the Wall of Fame. This wall holds 8 × 10 portraits of those regulars who have gone on before us. We pick at one another about who will be next to go on the wall and which one of the items off the menu was the culprit that put them up there.

There are several stories told during the morning as well as other times of the day. One patron will tell a story this week that was told by another patron last week, and it is similar but definitely has been changed to the liking of the one that is telling it this time. But no matter, everybody listens and laughs at the joke. I guess some are laughing at the change that has been made while others are laughing because they think it's funny that they already know the truth about the story. I have been eating in this restaurant for years and years. There have been many, many great storytellers that have sat and told them. Mr. Bill Johnson, a local historian and county commissioner, was as good as I have ever had the pleasure to listen to. He could so expertly insert something funny into his story. If I were eating and he started telling something, I made sure that I didn't have any food or drink in my mouth for fear of spewing it across the table. He has gone on before us, leaving it up to others who get to tell their stories at Table 8.

Vivian McClain is the owner of "Jakes." It was left to her by her father Jake and has done an excellent job of carrying on the tradition of good country cooking and some specialties that are a deviation of some of the items on the main menu. One of the favorites is the huge, delicious, everything-on-it-and-then-some Jake's Burger. Vivian is a very laid-back person that never gets upset about anything. When something happens out of the ordinary that proposes a problem, her main response is, "Oh well!" See what I mean? Vivian has donated to so, so many local functions and has stayed open after normal working hours to accommodate people who are running from hurricanes, tornadoes, and other trying times that may have come about. From this, Vivian was recently inducted into the Washington County Hall of Fame, which she so deserved.

I have a few stories that were told in Jakes that I would like to share with you.

Wayne—a young lady was utilizing her skills as a seamstress. She worked diligently cutting patterns and sewing together a pretty brightly colored dress. As she was proudly wearing it out one day, a gentleman noticed it and remarked, "Young lady, that is a beautiful dress you are wearing today!" She smiled and with bright eyes said, "Well, thank you very much. I made it myself." The gentleman replied, "I thought it looked homemade!"

Randy—when I was at the driver's license testing center, I was taking my written exam before taking my road test. Across the table from me, a testing officer was giving a test orally because the client could not read or write. I was listening intently to some of the questions and answers that were taking place. The officer came to this question: "When does one see a solid yellow line on the inside of the center dotted line on the roadway?" The client twisted and turned in his chair and put his face in his hands while trying his best to answer. I already knew it was at curves, hills, intersections, and no-pass zones. All of a sudden, the client's face lit up. I was thinking he finally had the answer. He was grinning from ear to ear and exclaimed, "About a hundred yards after you hit the main blacktop!"

Chuck—a man walked into a bar one day while dragging a six-foot heavy chain. He walks up to the bar, lifts the chain onto the bar, and orders a whiskey. The bartender pours him a drink. The man drinks it, drags the chain off the bar, and out the bar he goes. The next day, at the same time, the man comes in again dragging the long heavy chain, lifts it onto the bar, and orders a whiskey. The bartender pours him another drink. The man drinks it, drags the chain off the bar, and out the door he goes. This goes on for several days. Finally, the bartender asks the man, "Excuse me, sir. May I ask why you always pull that chain with you?" The man gives him a funny look and replies, "Well, I sure as hell can't PUSH it!"

About the Author

RANDY O'NEAL WAS BORN in 1948 to a family of God-fearing Southern Baptist parents and six older brothers and sisters. His father always worked long hours to provide for the family, farming and cutting timber for sawmills. His mother managed all other aspects of the large household, including handing out discipline whenever the need arose. Their love and hard work inspired Randy to want to tell of his growing up as a country boy in South Alabama. Randy worked many years in management at a large poultry company and retired after fifty years in 2017. He now owns a lawn service and is also a chauffeur for his grandchildren. He and his wife, Jean, live in Chatom, Alabama.

Printed in the USA
CPSIA information can be obtained
at www.ICGtesting.com
CBHW070852090724
11222CB00043B/730